ZTC
THE FIRST BRITISH DCC CONTROLLER MANUFACTURER... AND STILL GOING STRONG!
OUR ALL NEW ZTC 612 MASTER CONTROLLER IS ON THE WAY!
HELPLINE OPEN 9AM-9PM (closed Mondays)
01823 327155
TAUNTON CONTROLS LTD
AF400858

What's inside...

8 — A LOVE FOR RAILWAYS

Were model railways in the blood or from growing up in the right era? Pete Waterman explains how his passion for railways started and how it led to a lifetime of modelling.

16 — MODELS AND LEISURE KITS

The chance to create a brand-new range of kits with Models and Leisure was an opportunity Pete Waterman couldn't resist, even with the music business taking over. He explains how Models and Leisure Castings was created.

24 — ACTON IN PICTURES

Acton was Pete Waterman's first exhibition layout. It made its debut in 1981 at the Oxford Model Railway Exhibition. We delve into the archive to illustrate this mixed gauge layout which recreated the final years of the GWR broad gauge in 4mm:1ft scale with 'EM' gauge track.

28

Bespoke Gauge 1 10mm:1ft models could have been the future for Leamington Spa.

40 PRESERVING THE ELECTRICS
From the first moment Pete Waterman saw one of the new West Coast AC electrics at the turn of the '60s, he was hooked which led him to preserve as many as possible of the original locomotive types. Pete explains how he came to save the AC electrics and how it has impacted his modelling.

50 JUST LIKE THE REAL THING
Just Like the Real Thing was created to bring 7mm scale modellers top quality, highly detailed kits. Pete Waterman explains how the company was created and the challenges it faced.

62 LEAMINGTON SPA
'O' gauge and Leamington Spa are what Pete Waterman is best known for in railway modelling. Pete Waterman introduces the layout and Mike Wild take a full tour of his amazing 'O' gauge model of Leamington Spa, Hatton Bank and Brinklow including previously unseen images.

74 LEAMINGTON UNDER CONSTRUCTION
We delve into Pete Waterman's archive of images to illustrate the early construction of Leamington Spa, Hatton Bank and Brinklow.

80 THE MAKING TRACKS STORY
Making Tracks burst onto the scene in 2021 with brand-new energy for the model railway scene. Pete Waterman explains the how the first three layouts came to be.

90 THE FINAL FRONTIER
Pete Waterman reflects on how a record-breaking layout helped steady the course of the UK model railway scene – reassuring manufacturers, inspiring modellers, and proving that teamwork, ambition and scenic detail still matter more than ever.

102 70 YEARS OF CHANGE
From gluing together kits in post-war Coventry to pioneering cutting-edge 'O' gauge models, Pete Waterman reflects on seven decades immersed in railway modelling. He shares how the hobby has evolved, what's been gained – and lost – along the way, and why Making Tracks marks both a proud milestone and a heartfelt connection to a lifelong passion.

Below: A lifetime of modelling! Pete Waterman holds up the Guinness World Records official certificate at Model World LIVE 2024 for Making Tracks - The Final Frontier.

28 BECOMING A COLLECTOR
With a booming music career time for modelling changed and while it never left Pete's mind new scales took his attention. Pete Waterman how and why he started collecting unique and special 'O' gauge and Gauge One locomotives.

34 ENTERING PRESERVATION
Modelling was all about capturing realism in miniature, but when Pete Waterman had the opportunity to own full size locomotives in preservation he jumped at the chance leading to a long-standing association with railway heritage including operating the first main line registered preserved diesel locomotive and restoring one of the unsung heroes of freight by rail. He explains how it all started.

Welcome...

Pete Waterman has spent a lifetime making models and connected to the full size railway. He leans from the cab of Class 47 47790 at Manchester station on April 13 2013 during a Northern Belle fund raising trip for 'When You Wish Upon a Star'. Tony Woolliscroft/WireImage/Getty Images.

If someone had told me, all those years ago standing on the platform at Leamington Spa with a pencil and notebook, that I'd still be just as fascinated with railways seventy years later - I probably would've smiled and said, "I hope so." Because the truth is, railways have never left me. They've shaped my life just as much as music has.

This book isn't about fame, record deals, or the pop charts. It's about something far more personal - a lifelong love affair with model railways. From my first Tri-ang locomotive in the 1950s to building layouts at sizes I could never have imagined, every bit of this journey has been driven by passion, curiosity and a sheer joy in bringing railways to life in miniature.

For me, model railways aren't just a hobby - they're a way of telling stories. Every model I've ever built, whether in 'OO', 'O' gauge, or something grander still, has been about capturing a moment in time, recreating the feeling I had as a kid watching with wonder as a GWR 'Castle' thundered through the station. It's that sense of wonder I've always tried to hold onto in all my modelling.

Over the decades, I've been lucky enough to build alongside some incredibly talented people, to discover their skills, create products, exhibit layouts that mean the world to me, and to keep learning - because that's what this hobby does. It keeps you thinking, solving, building. It keeps you young.

This special publication is a look back, yes, but it's also a celebration of what makes railway modelling so special. The camaraderie. The craftsmanship. The sheer magic of seeing something you built from scratch come to life when the power goes on and the locomotive rolls.

Whether you're just getting started or have been in the game longer than me, I hope there's something in here that makes you smile, nod in recognition, or feel inspired to get back to the workbench.

Thanks for coming along for the ride - it's been a fantastic journey.

Pete Waterman OBE

ISBN: 978 1 83632 136 1
Editor: Mike Wild
Author: Pete Waterman
Senior editor, specials: Paul Sander
Email: paul.sander@keypublishing.com
Design: Panda Media
Advertising Sales Manager: Sam Clark
Email: sam.clark@keypublishing.com
Tel: 01780 755131
Advertising Production: Becky Antoniades
Email: Rebecca.antoniades@keypublishing.com

SUBSCRIPTION/MAIL ORDER
Key Publishing Ltd, PO Box 300, Stamford,
Lincs, PE9 1NA
Tel: 01780 480404

Subscriptions email: subs@keypublishing.com
Mail Order email: orders@keypublishing.com
Website: www.keypublishing.com/shop

PUBLISHING
Group CEO: Adrian Cox
Publisher: Steve O'Hara

PUBLISHED BY
Key Publishing Ltd, PO Box 100, Stamford, Lincs, PE9 1XQ
Tel: 01780 755131 Website: www.keypublishing.com

PRINTING
Precision Colour Printing Ltd, Haldane,
Halesfield 1, Telford, Shropshire. TF7 4QQ

DISTRIBUTION
Seymour Distribution Ltd, 2 Poultry Avenue,
London, EC1A 9PU. **Enquiries Line:** 02074 294000.

A love for railways

Were model railways in the blood or from growing up in the right era? **PETE WATERMAN** explains how his passion for railways started and how it led to a lifetime of modelling.

What a different world it was back in the 1950s when I took up trainspotting. Just a few years after the Second World War, Britain was very grey and run-down - there were bombed buildings everywhere. My dad still worked 47 hours a week, including Saturday mornings, and to say money was tight would be an understatement. That said, my mum was a housewife, and I had a younger sister.

We had an aunty who lived outside Rugby and another who lived in a posh part of Coventry. We visited my aunty in Coventry on Tuesdays and met my aunty in Rugby most Wednesdays. We lived with my grandad, but dad never got home until after six. It was my grandad who got me into railways, as he used to go for long walks every day, usually ending up at a local pub to play dominoes. But he would always stop near a railway line to watch the trains go by. In fact, his house was very close to the line to Coventry Colliery, so I guess I was born to the sound of steam engines passing by.

It was my grandad who bought me my first train set for Christmas 1948 - a clockwork engine and two coaches on a circle of track. My dad and grandad had gone to watch Coventry City play Northampton Town in Northampton, and the bus had stopped outside a toy shop. I can still see that set going round the dinner table even today.

There were no railway workers in my family, so I didn't understand why I'd caught the railway bug, but I had. My grandad had a good Army pension from the First World War. I've never been able to find out why, as his Army records were destroyed in the Second World War. In fact, when I was asked to do the TV show Who Do You Think You Are, I found out a lot more about him, but there was still a question over the pension. While researching for a Radio 2 documentary for Remembrance Day, the War Museum told me that soldiers of the First World War didn't get pensions! I insisted he had one, so they checked their database, and yes, I was right. He had been retired with a pension. We couldn't find out why, but they said it was very, very unusual.

I later discovered that my great grandad on my dad's side had been a driver on the Great Northern Railway, so maybe it really was in the blood somewhere along the line?

BECOMING A SPOTTER

It was the visits to my mum's sisters that made me a spotter. As I've already said, things were so different back in the early fifties. When we went to Rugby to see my aunty Else, it was market day. I was left at the station until the afternoon, so I spent hours

With a heavy load of iron ore behind, GWR Collett '2884' 3850 glides into the centre road at Leamington Spa with a feather of steam at the safety valves in May 1960. This location was one of Pete Waterman's primary spotting locations in the 1950s.
G Parry Collection/Colour Rail.

> *"Great Western engines had me hooked, if I wasn't already... with their deep green colour, brass and copper - wow!"*
>
> **PETE WATERMAN**

watching trains, right up to the age I started school. And because I was born in 1947, along with millions of others, I couldn't get a school place until 1954.

On Tuesdays we always visited my Aunty Jenne. During the summer, my uncle Erne would go fishing on the River Leam in Leamington Spa, and we'd go and take him his lunch. We always travelled by train. Just like visits to Rugby they would leave me at the station, and pick me up after lunch. The Great Western engines had me hooked, if I wasn't already. Apart from the blue 'Duchesses' and 'Princesses' by Stanier, the rest were black. The GWR engines, with their deep green colour, brass and copper - wow! And they all seemed to have names, it was another world.

You can see by now that beer plays an important part in my life as those early trips out were connected to grandad heading out to play dominos, and I'm not even a drinker! One of the things that made a difference was my mate Keith's dad. He was a toolmaker and had a workshop in his garage. He had steam engines that ran on spirits, planes with small petrol engines, and racing cars powered by the same engines. Boy, did they shift!

It was Keith's dad, Ron, who was really interested in trains. He had a fabulous old Triumph. During the summer, after tea, he would go fishing and ask if my dad wanted to join him. We always went to Brinklow, where the canal runs next to the railway. I guess he could fish and watch the trains at the same time. I can't remember him writing anything down, and of course, there was The Railway, a pub on the bridge over the station. Yes, beer again! And out the back window you could watch the trains go by.

Looking back, I can see Ron was far keener than Keith was. In those days you weren't allowed in pubs under 14, we were nowhere near that, so we'd hang around the station. The station had been closed for some time, but the signalbox was still open, and there was a gate in the pub car park next to the chicken hutch!

The thing about Brinklow is that there's a curve before the platform, and the engines were at full speed when they hit the start of the ramp. The noise was fantastic as expresses hurtled through the station. What I remember most about the summer nights at Brinklow was how still it all was, that was until you heard the signal

go up, then the roar of the engine. The engines that made the most noise were the Liverpool trains hauled by the Stanier 'Princess Royals'. I can still see them to this day.

The station buildings were above the track, and as the engines shot under them, the blast from the chimney made dust fall from the closed station. When the train had gone, you could see dust drifting from the buildings in the fading sunlight. It was magic.

Then one evening, still such a strong memory, Ron, Keith's dad (Uncle Ron to me; back then everyone in the family or close friends were uncles or aunts) asked if I wanted to go with him and Keith to Brinklow to see a special train, or engine, as it turned out,

Instead of fishing, just spotting. That told me Uncle Ron was more interested than he let on.

The reason? The English Electric prototype 'Deltic' in its striking blue livery was pulling its first train. It had been in the papers! Was Ron a secret *Railway Magazine* reader? He even knew what time it would be at Brinklow. That tells you everything.

So that night, instead of a Liverpool, we saw the 'Deltic' – the first of its kind, making its first appearance on the West Coast Main Line at Brinklow. As we stood on the closed platform at Brinklow, we heard the roar, and as it came around the curve the driver sounded the horn and waved. If I wasn't a fanatic before, I was now.

Main: Seeing the prototype 'Deltic' on its first trip on the West Coast Main Line was a true moment for Pete Waterman. Now in service on May 25 1957, the striking blue locomotive charges through Watford Junction with the Down 'Shamrock'. *CRL Coles/Rail Archive Stephenson.*

Below: Coventry was an inspiration for Pete Waterman's modelling. Seeing the city and the railway rebuilt in the 1960s drew his attention to the world around the railway. Carlisle based rebuilt 'Patriot' 4-6-0 45545 *Planet* waits to depart Coventry on October 23 1963. *Neville Simms/Ranwell Collection/Railphotoprints.uk.*

Brinklow was an important place in Pete Waterman's early spotting days. Located alongside the Oxford Canal, the station had already closed by the time he started visiting. Representing the period, 'Royal Scot' 4-6-0 46156 *The South Wales Borderer* runs alongside the Oxford Canal near Shilton, to the north of Brinklow, with a northbound van train on September 20 1963. *Neville Simms/Ranwell Collection/Railphotoprints.uk.*

CLASSROOM SPOTTING

Yes, when you're that young, the summer school holidays are never long enough. The sun seemed to shine every day, and as long as you had a bottle of water, you could stay out all day, only reporting back for tea.

But life was about to change. I was old enough to go to senior school, and this was when I was supposed to start taking life seriously, as in four years I'd be looking for a job. But with a classroom window that looked out onto the railway line, I spent more time looking out than at books. If I liked a subject, I paid attention, often more than the rest of the class. This is where railways really helped. I excelled in Geography, History and Maths – and that's because I had an *ABC Combine*! The Stanier 'Jubilees' were named after Commonwealth countries, admirals, and warships. Teachers were shocked when I knew where Fiji was, or who Rodney was. See, railways do have an educational connection.

It was at school that the spotting really started. There were lots of lads who would swap numbers, and that changed my railway interest from then on. But it was always the railway, not just the numbers, that I was passionate about.

LMS 3P 2-6-2T 40009 departs from Leamington Avenue station on the Midland route with a Birmingham New Street-Rugby train on February 19 1949. *John P Wilson/Rail Archive Stephenson.*

BECOMING A MODELLER

Growing up in Coventry, I was surrounded by bombed-out buildings. This was especially true at the station and in the city centre. It fascinated me. I never wanted just a train set, I wanted mine to look like the real thing, in all its detail. As the station was being rebuilt, it was as much about the scaffolding as the trains. It was that level of detail I wanted in my layouts.

In search of detail I soon turned my attention to the locomotives and coaches. This was around 1956. No one around me was really into models like I was, but wait a minute, Keith's dad seemed to know more than he let on. He built Keith a Trix train set, mounted it on a board with a station, signals and points. That was my way in.

He took a magazine, I can't remember what it was called, but I would borrow it and spend hours looking through it. That was the start.

The first thing I learned was that serious modellers used 'EM' gauge! I was a serious modeller, or so I thought, so there was to be no third rail, and the gauge had to be 18mm. Sounds easy when you say it like that, but remember this was the mid-1950s when model railways in Britain were still driven by Hornby Dublo alongside Tri-ang and Trix.

Never one to let a lack of tools stop me, I went ahead. There were two model shops in Coventry. In those days, many shops sold Hornby, Tri-ang and Trix, but only two sold bits and pieces. I soon found that a few people would spend time chatting in those model shops, and even though I was a young kid with limited pocket money, they answered my questions and showed me how they did things.

With my limited tools, I began improving my stock. I started building Peco wagons that fitted on Tri-ang wagon chassis. One of the shops sold 'EM' gauge wheels that fitted so I was away, modelling on a very tight budget.

After a year of building them and learning about glue (I still don't know why), I took a couple into show the shop owner. He clearly remembered me, he'd sold me the kits, and

PETE WATERMAN

I was surprised when he said he really liked them. He even said he could sell them if I wanted the money! So we struck a deal: he gave me the wagons and wheels, and I got bits and pieces I needed in return.

In the early 1960s, Kitmaster began making plastic railway kits. That was it for me, I was now in a position to turn down modelling work and still have spare cash for tools and more.

At the time, I still lived with Mum, Dad and my sister, so I had no space for a layout and did all my modelling on the kitchen table. Of course, there comes a point in all our lives when time is short. Football, girls, and music became important to me, but I still kept modelling.

In its last weeks of service GWR Collett 'King' 4-6-0 6016 *King Edward V* calls at Leamington Spa with a Paddington-Wolverhampton service in July 1962. This location was another regular visit for Pete Waterman as a young trainspotter. The location gave him the connection of Great Western Railway motive power as well as providing the location for his 'O' gauge layout. *Railphotoprints.uk.*

I'd always been interested in German aeroplanes, so I started building Airfix and other model planes. One strong memory was building a Heinkel He 111 while watching England win the World Cup in 1966.

I also built a lot of Mk 1 coaches for a guy at the model shop. I could never make enough and they were all Kitmaster kits. Then I saw one that had been kit bashed into a type of Mk 1 for which there was no kit. That led me to do the same, a new market!

KITMASTER

When the locomotive kits came out, there was a market for fitting motors and adding detail. I had become a pretty competent plastic modeller, but this meant using metal for the chassis. Back then, the standard was 1/8in brass. I had to cut them out, drill the holes for the wheels, and fit bushes. You could buy all this at the model shop. The wheels were made by Hamblings, and you got as close as you could to the size you needed!

Being a mad GWR fan, the Kitmaster kit for Churchward GWR 'City' 4-4-0 3440 *City of Truro* was a godsend - everybody wanted one, so I always had a list. I remember once having a cupboard with a dozen kits to build. I had loads of books on GWR locomotives, and 4-4-0s were a big part of their fleet. I used that kit as a base to start building other 4-4-0s. The model shop sold thin nickel silver sheet, and so it began, as I worked my way through creation of unique models to build my collection and offer to others.

Reading based GWR 'Castle' 4-6-0 5076 *Gladiator* leaves Leamington Spa with an Inter-Regional service for the South Coast on July 29 1962. On the left the GWR lower quadrant semaphore signals can be seen while on the right are Midland Region upper quadrants for the line through Avenue station. *Neville Simms/Railphotoprints.uk.*

I remember being sold a book on how to build model locomotives. After reading it again and again, I bought a pair of jewellers' shears. Once I learned how to use flux properly, the world was my oyster.

At that time, I was working as a telephone engineer for GEC in the Exchange Division as a mechanical engineer. This meant I had lots of tools that helped with modelling, and I had to do a lot of soldering, which had to pass GPO inspection, so it had to be top quality.

I was now an avid reader of all the model railway press, always looking for tips. Most people I worked with knew about my hobby. One day, during a conversation in the exchange, a guy said he had an old train set at home, did I want it? His kids had no interest. He gave me a Graham Farish 'OO' gauge Stanier 'Black Five' 4-6-0 which was tender-

A grimy Ivatt '2MT' 2-6-2T ambles through Leamington Spa with a short northbound parcels train on June 20 1964. The lower level Avenue station can be seen on the left of the GWR lower quadrant signals. *Neville Simms/ Ranwell Collection/Railphotoprints.uk.*

The trainshed roof at Rugby offered brilliant atmosphere, especially in the days of steam. On July 31 1963 Stanier 'Black Five' 44833 simmers in the bay platform after arrival from London Euston. *Railphotoprints.uk.*

The structure of Rugby trainshed breaks up the light over BR 'Britannia' 70004 *William Shakespeare* as it heads south through Rugby with a mixed freight on May 23 1964. This was one of the locations that Pete Waterman enjoyed many hours at in his early years watching and spotting the final years of steam as the new wave of diesel and electric traction arrived on the scene. *Neville Simms/Ranwell Collection/Railphotoprints.uk.*

driven. I'd never seen one before. By the standards of the day, it was a fantastic model and although I was a GWR modeller, I thought I'd spend some time bringing it into line with the era I was modelling.

I had a Badger airbrush by now and sprayed all my models, but I'd never hand-lined, always using transfers. Then one of those chance meetings - that seem to be the story of my life - happened. In one of the magazines, I saw some photographs of GWR Ratio kits. They were 1900s four-wheeled full brakes, kit-bashed from standard kits. In the same article was a South African scratch-built locomotive. The builder was a guy called Ron Cadman.

I had a workbench in the wiring shop at the GEC Stoke, Coventry factory. If there were any mechanical faults, I was there to sort them - broken tags were the big issue. A lady who sat behind my bench came over and said to me, "My son has some photographs in that magazine." Really? Her name was Ada Cadman. The penny didn't drop at first. I asked where he got his bits from, and it turned out to be the

same shop I used so I made arrangements to meet him there.

Ron was a fantastic modeller and a production engineer at Jaguar Cars. We talked, and he showed me a GWR Collett 'King' 4-6-0 that was in the glass case, waiting to be picked up by a customer. It was fantastic, the lining was spot-on. I asked him how he did it, and he invited me to his workshop to show me.

It was the first time I had seen a bow pen, let alone used one. He showed me how to mix the paint and the trick with talcum powder for getting into the crevices of the model. I had the perfect model to try it on: my Farish 'Black Five'. I felt I could strip and respray this more easily than one of my GWR locomotives.

I took my time, added boiler bands in the way he showed me (made from cigarette paper), and I was knocked out with the results. I thought I'd show it to Ron for feedback. Guessing he'd be in the shop on Saturday, I took it down, but he had been there the night before.

"What was I wanting to show him?" they asked. So I took out the 'Black Five'. The lady, who was the shop owner's wife, asked if I could hang about as her husband was on his way in. I wasn't in a rush.

When he turned up, he looked at it and said, "Do you want to sell it? It's good." I wasn't sure I did, this was my first lining job. "I can give you £40 cash, or £50 in goods." Done!

The first white metal kits were just starting to appear on the market around the late 1960s. With the money, I bought a K's GWR 'Bulldog', wheels, motor and a low-melt soldering iron. At the time, Araldite was the glue used in kit building, but I could never get on with it and superglues were only just arriving. People used to cure the Araldite in the oven. I've seen so many blobs of white metal that started off as kits as it was easy to overheat them and cause the white metal to return to its original form!

The kits of this period were pretty basic and needed a lot of work, and I mean a lot. But there was nothing else of high standard to build. The first kits that changed everything were from Wills, they upped the game. The white metal was in a different class in a Wills kit.

Looking back to the late 1960s and early '70s, there were some poor model kits on the market. In some cases you couldn't even say they were a basis for scratchbuilding.

By this time, my music career was taking off, and I was in a position to buy my first house, which had a spare bedroom I could use as a modelling den (still no room for a layout). The two shops that sold railway bits had closed, and a new one opened - all about model railways – called Models and Leisure. It was on the other side of Coventry, but it became a Mecca, and every Saturday you'd find me there. Ron was just round the corner, so he popped in most weeks.

Barry Jones, who owned the shop, was a builder and an 'O' gauge modeller. I was still modelling in 'EM' at that time. One of the regulars, about my age, did work for the shop. It turned out he turned Barry's 'O' gauge wheels and made his chimneys. My big problem in modelling was that I had no lathe or the skill to use one. So I asked if he'd do some 4mm wheels for me. His name was Chris Louth, and it was the start of a friendship that lasted over 50 years.

Looking back, it was Chris who got me into 'O' gauge. CCW made kits in stamped-out nickel silver. I bought a 'Pannier', Chris got a 'Small Prairie' and that was the start. Chris turned the wheels, I did the painting. He built a loop in his loft so we could run them which started another adventure in modelling with a new layout project about to begin. ■

Guy Williams modelling at Pendon was an inspiration to Pete Waterman for the detail, accuracy and operation of his 'EM' gauge locomotives. On the Dartmoor layout, which dates back to 1955, a GWR '28XX' 2-8-0 leads an 80 wagon coal train across Walkham Viaduct. Models capable of this level of performance and reality were what Pete wanted to achieve. *Mike Wild.*

Models and Leisure Castings was a collaboration between Pete Waterman, Barry Jones and Ron Cadman. One of the most successful was the joint boxing of a GWR '850' 0-6-0ST and a '633' 0-6-0T to the same price point as a tender locomotive. *Hattons Model Railways Archive.*

Models and leisure kits

The chance to create a brand-new range of kits with Models and Leisure was an opportunity **PETE WATERMAN** couldn't resist, even with the music business taking over. He explains how Models and Leisure Castings was created.

By now, the music business was taking over my life, but I was still home every weekend and as my career took off I finally had the money to do what I had always wanted: rebuild my house. It was two cottages knocked into one, with a good-sized garden front and back. Part of it went back 300 years, and it was in pretty bad shape. That's where the bathroom was and, in the winter, well, say no more.

Models and Leisure model shop owner Barry Jones, being a builder, rebuilt the house and extended it with a big kitchen, two extra bedrooms, an upstairs bathroom, and most importantly, a large workshop to model in.

I joined the GWR Broad Gauge Society - I think my membership number was 2 - along with Ian Rice and a few others. Shows were changing. The big factor here was Pendon - it had such a huge impact on us all. Guy Williams' locomotives were out of this

world and were leading the way when it came to detail, accuracy and operation. The magazines were full of Pendon as the models of Dartmoor and the Vale Scene took centre stage. I was bitten by the bug.

By now, OPC in Oxford had become the home of the BR archive of drawings. They had published GWR Engines Parts 1 and 2, so I now had drawings for pretty much any GWR locomotive I wanted to build. Along with the RCTS books and the first coach books by John Lewis (who I knew very well), I felt confident enough to start building a layout.

I was in the shop one Saturday when Barry asked if I ever went near Bristol. As it happened, that was part of my patch in the music industry. There had been an advert for what looked like a shop selling kits for a GWR 'County' and 'Manor' 4-6-0. Barry gave me the money and asked me to pick him up one of each. I said yes, and decided to get one of each for myself as well.

It was around 1 o'clock when I got to the address. It wasn't far from BBC Bristol, but when I arrived, I realised it wasn't a shop, it was a house. I knocked on the door and, in no uncertain terms, got told where to go. I was shocked. I'd double-checked the name and address. Later, I found out from both Guy Williams and Tony Reynolds that this wasn't an unusual response. And his kits? Well, best not to say.

MEET RON

The following Saturday, Barry asked me to pick up some kits from a workshop in Leicester - Leek & Manifold Railway narrow gauge kits. I often did things like this while travelling around the country (remember, this was before sat navs - just a map on your knee!). I found the building and the workshop was on the second floor - this time I was ready for whatever might happen.

There was a trade counter with a lady behind it, and in the background, a man

Models and Leisure Castings' first kit was the GWR 'Manor' 4-6-0 closely followed by the Hawksworth 'County'. The kits were designed to be built and used white metal for the bodies together with an etched brass chassis. *Hattons Model Railway Archive.*

wearing an apron using a blowtorch. 'That's different,' I thought. I said I'd come to pick up an order for Models and Leisure, Coventry.

"Oh, come in. Cup of tea? Ron, do you want one?"

"Yeah, go on then."

Like so many things in my life, it started my brain ticking. I could see the guy was soldering brass parts together. It turned out he was a pattern maker. He had made all the patterns in the kit and others I recognised. "Do you do any patterns for GWR locomotives?" I asked. "Yeah, I could do that."

I went away with a half-formed idea in my head. The pattern maker was Ron Cadman, and after a conversation with Barry I invited him to come and talk to us about doing some work. He said he and a few others had their castings made by a guy in Leicester. He gave me a price. I said yes - we'd start with the patterns for a GWR 'Manor'. "Book me a slot when you're ready."

It wasn't all plain sailing though, and I needed more input than Barry could give right away, so I spoke to Ron in more detail, after all, he was a production engineer, and the three of us formed Models and Leisure Kits.

From day one, I had a clear idea of what I wanted for this new venture: a kit that went together as easily as an Airfix plastic kit but made from whitemetal and brass. Not too many parts, but all the essential details - including a full backhead, brakes, and the big new thing at the time: an etched chassis. It had to be to scale and capable of accepting a motor and gearbox. The boiler and firebox were in two parts, the footplate in one. It was made to be built.

When we got the first castings, Ron and I put one together. There were a few problems - not with the patterns, but with the casting quality. It didn't take long before we realised we'd have to bite the bullet and set up our

own casting workshop to be able to reach the standard that we wanted.

Ron had just left Jaguar and gone to Lucas Batteries which was perfect timing, as he was setting up their new casting factory in Ireland. That gave us access to a company that made white metal. Lucas was a massive company, and their rep was a model railway fan. They worked with us on removing lead from the white metal and improving the casting process. Although we only had a small unit, we were turning out fantastic castings and easy-to-build kits.

We priced them competitively, and with a strong first review under our belt, the orders poured in. We soon started work on our next kit: the GWR 'County' 4-6-0 along the same lines as the 'Manor'. Some weeks, when I drove to London, I hated to think how much weight I was carrying in the car considering how many kits and parts were in the boot.

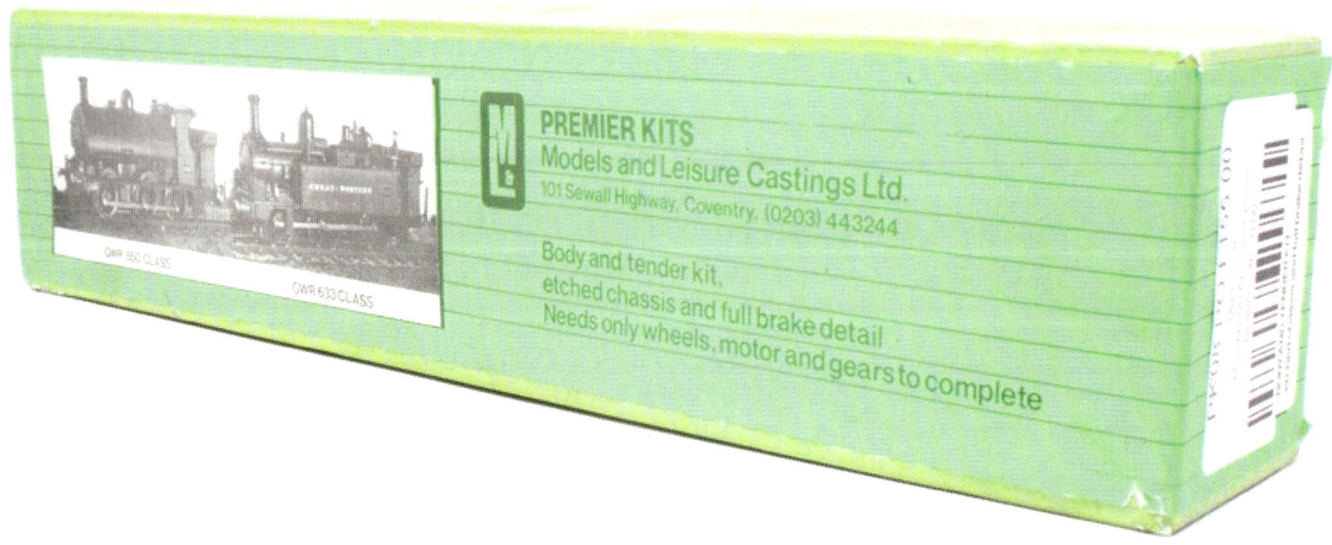

The twin pack featuring the GWR '850' 0-6-0ST and '633' 0-6-0T was a brilliant step for Models and Leisure. They couldn't make enough when the kit emerged on to the market. *Hattons Model Railway Archive.*

The final years of the GWR broad gauge and in particular the mixed gauge operation were the basis for Pete Waterman's first exhibition layout. In this 1900 period drawing from the Century Edition of Cassell's History of England, a GWR broad gauge train enters Acton alongside a GWR '850' 0-6-0ST. *Universal History Archive/Universal Images Group via Getty Images.*

We couldn't keep up. We had to start working in shifts. I did the shows with Ron, and sometimes we'd have to go back to Coventry mid-show to pick up more kits to keep up with demand.

So what next? We'd picked the two big gaps in the market. Both were tender locomotives. I weighed the kits, tender and locomotive, and they were almost identical. So, why not do two tank engines in one box, for the same price as a tender locomotive? And they had to be different GWR types to stay on theme: an '850' 0-6-0ST and a '633' 0-6-0T.

There were a few raised eyebrows as it was seen as completely out of the ordinary. Some dealers were pessimistic. I wasn't. And if the first two kits had done well, they were nothing compared to the tanks. People were swapping with each other, even placing adverts in the magazines for trades. Fantastic. We continued to develop the range and created sought after models of Churchward's unique 'Pacific' *The Great Bear* as well as LNWR locomotives including dock tanks, 2-4-2Ts and a Ramsbottom 'Special' 0-6-0ST.

SHOWPIECE

Doing the shows, I saw a gap and had the idea to build a portable layout. Barry was still rebuilding my house, so there was plenty of space. Being so into Broad Gauge, and with few layouts or models about, I was fascinated by the idea of building a new railway in 4mm scale recreating those final years of the 7ft 1/4in Great Western Railway operations.

To be honest, I wasn't just a Broad Gauge fan, but I was a Mixed Gauge fan. The 1890s photographs always fascinated me, so it had to be mixed gauge, 1890s.

At that point, there were no track standards, no rolling stock, and no locomotives. The leading light in the society was Eddy Brown, who lived in Rugby which made him easy to visit. Then there was John Lewis who was a fountain of knowledge on wagons and coaches who I could meet in London at lunchtime. David Hide from the Met would pop in too. My office was on Hyde Park Corner which made it easy for others to visit. Now I had the information, a team, and a place.

Another kit in the range was for the GWR's only 4-6-2 – *The Great Bear*. This part build kit shows the main components of the model. *Hattons Model Railway Archive.*

Images of the final years of broad gauge operation were a huge inspiration to Pete Waterman's model of Acton in 'EM' gauge. A Great Western Broad Gauge 'Single' passes through Sonning Cutting near Reading around 1890 illustrating the mixed gauge track of the period.
Rail Photo/Construction Photography/Avalon/Getty Images.

I chose Acton in West London as the setting for the new layout set in the last week of mixed gauge operation. That also allowed me to add the North London Line. I went to Acton with a tape measure and a camera and was shocked how little had changed since the Broad Gauge era.

At the time, all my locomotives and stock were painted by Brian Badger in Birmingham, who gave me the phone numbers of a couple of guys he thought could help. Over dinner one Saturday night, I talked him into helping me directly to get the layout off the ground.

After speaking with Gerry Beale at OPC, I was invited to take Acton to the Oxford show the next year. The only problem was, at that point, I had no layout, no rolling stock, no track, and about a year to build it all. Oh, and by the way, I had never wired a layout before.

One thing I'm definitely not is a carpenter, as Dave Douglas from the Railnuts would testify. But off I went, with the idea of a storage yard at each end and the station in the middle. The boards were 6ft wide and 12ft long, a total of 48ft. The concept included an Up and Down fast line in mixed gauge, an Up and Down slow line in standard gauge, and an Up and Down North London line.

At the time, most layouts were quite low, so you looked down on them. I felt this wasn't the best way to view a model railway. So we, or rather I, decided to raise it to 4ft off the ground. Looking back, I can't even work out how we managed it. But by the time the show came around, I had just enough stock to make it work, including the Royal Train.

In truth, the broad gauge engines were thin on the ground, but the two broad gauge 0-4-4Ts were up to the task. All the track was scratch-built from square strips soldered onto nickel silver. All the buildings were made from plastic card. Brian Caldecott from Bob's Models in Birmingham wired the point motors and sorted out the electrics. I did the rest of the wiring.

Brian said we needed some trees, as there were lots visible in the photographs of Acton from the 1890s. He showed me how to make them, and I'm still making trees like those today. They're hard work, but there's a great joy in completing one.

FIRST SHOW

So, to the Oxford show! What I haven't mentioned yet is that, at this moment, my music career was also taking off. I'd just had my first number one hit - Pass the Dutchie by Musical Youth. I borrowed their van to get the layout to the show would you believe!

Chris Louth came along as an operator and co-pilot. It was only when we had to load the van that reality hit. The boards weighed a ton and the show was in the town hall, up two flights of stairs! Chris was out on his feet; he didn't have the bulk I did.

We showed Acton a couple more times, but I decided I wanted to build a permanent layout, properly. There was an old cowshed at the back of my house, so I bought it along with a strip of land that went with it. I extended the garden to include it, rebuilt the shed, and turned it into a proper railway room.

I built the baseboards and started on what I hoped would be my perfect layout. I got a lot done, but by now the music business had taken over my life, and I could no longer live in Coventry. Instead of building model railways, I found myself building music studios. ■

The broad gauge era was altogether different. Marking the last 7ft 1/4in gauge train to depart London Paddingon in 1892, the final 177 miles of track were converted to standard 4ft 8 1/2in gauge in just two days! *SSPL/Getty Images.*

A Models and Leisure GWR '633' 0-6-0T poses with the permanent way gang on Pete Waterman's 'EM' gauge model of Acton. *Pete Waterman Archive.*

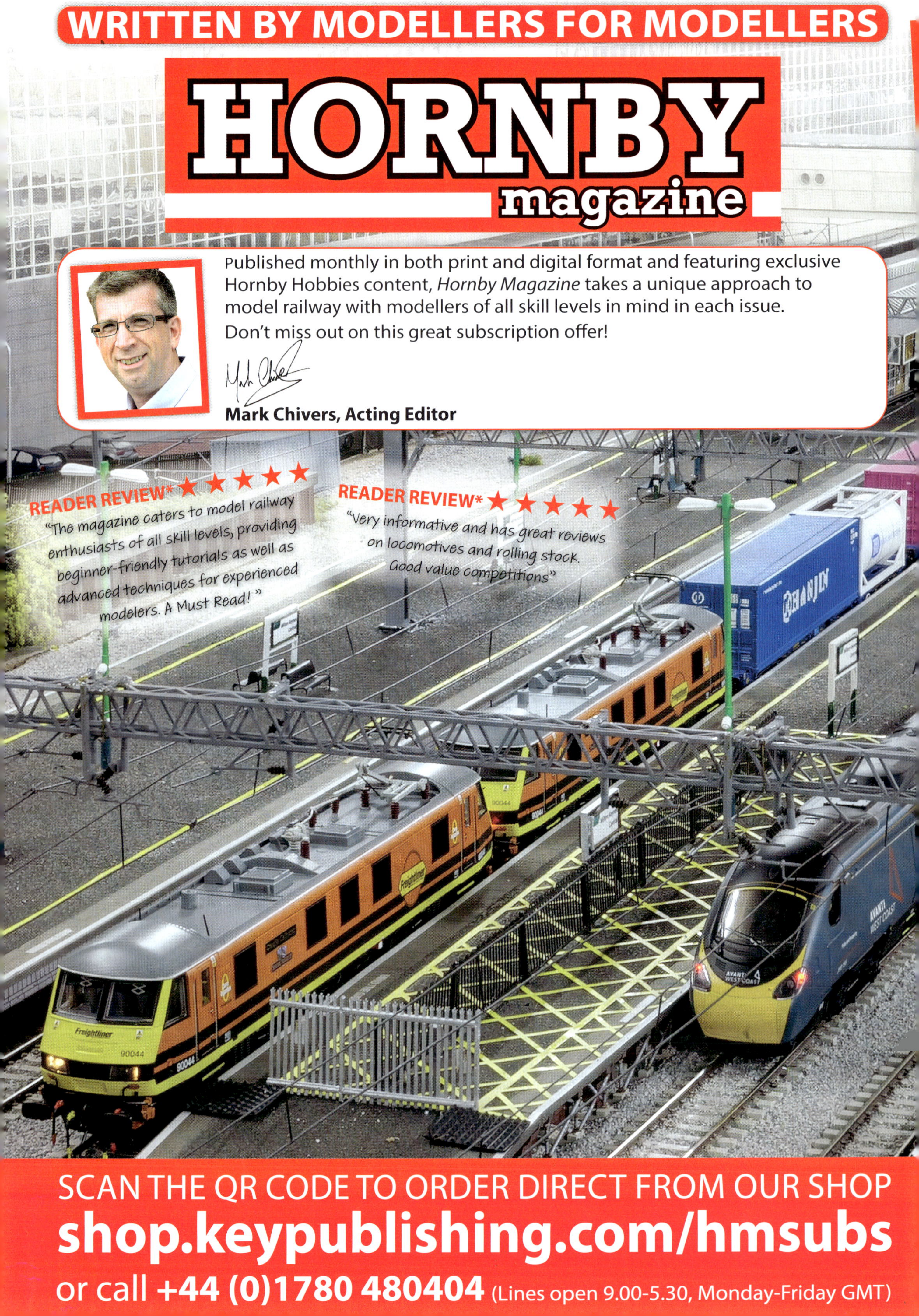
WRITTEN BY MODELLERS FOR MODELLERS
HORNBY
magazine
Published monthly in both print and digital format and featuring exclusive Hornby Hobbies content, Hornby Magazine takes a unique approach to model railway with modellers of all skill levels in mind in each issue.
Don't miss out on this great subscription offer!
Mark Chivers, Acting Editor
READER REVIEW* ★★★★★
"The magazine caters to model railway enthusiasts of all skill levels, providing beginner-friendly tutorials as well as advanced techniques for experienced modelers. A Must Read!"
READER REVIEW* ★★★★★
"Very informative and has great reviews on locomotives and rolling stock. Good value competitions"
SCAN THE QR CODE TO ORDER DIRECT FROM OUR SHOP
shop.keypublishing.com/hmsubs
or call +44 (0)1780 480404 (Lines open 9.00-5.30, Monday-Friday GMT)

SUBSCRIBE TODAY!

WHICH *HORNBY MAGAZINE* SUBSCRIPTION SUITS YOU BEST?

A **12 MONTH SUBSCRIPTION** *BEST VALUE*

UK PRINT - 1 year

£65.99

Paying by Credit or Debit card

FREE GIFT INCLUDED!

B **6 MONTH SUBSCRIPTION**

UK PRINT - 6 months

£32.99

Paying by Credit or Debit Card

SAVE 50P PER ISSUE!

FREE GIFT

WORTH £34.00!

Receive a **FREE pair of tickets** to

Reader reviews from Pocketmags

GWR 'Queen' 2-2-2 1132 *Prince of Wales* passes through the crossovers on the standard gauge lines alongside a GWR Armstrong '633' 0-6-0T with permanent way vans. *Pete Waterman Archive.*

Acton in pictures

Acton was **PETE WATERMAN'S** first exhibition layout. It made its debut in 1983 at the Oxford Model Railway Exhibition. We delve into the archive to illustrate this mixed gauge layout which recreated the final year of the GWR broad gauge in 4mm:1ft scale with 'EM' gauge track.

GWR 'Dean Single' 4-2-2 3047 *Lorna Doone* pauses in Acton station on the standard gauge lines. All the locomotives for Acton were built to 'EM' gauge standards. *Pete Waterman Archive.*

Modelling the early GWR standard gauge locomotives called for scratchbuilding and new Models and Leisure kits. GWR 'Queen' 2-2-2 3011 Greyhound pauses in the platforms at Acton. *Pete Waterman Archive.*

A Rhymney Railway 0-6-2T makes a rare visitor to Acton on a passenger working. *Pete Waterman Archive.*

'Queen' 2-2-2 1132 *Prince of Wales* stops on the station to show its outside springs on the locomotive and tender. Etched brass and whitemetal were the material choices of the day for these models. *Pete Waterman Archive.*

Left: A GWR '850' 0-6-0ST – part of the Models and Leisure Kits twin pack with a '633' 0-6-0T – passes the signalbox at the end of Acton's platforms. *Pete Waterman Archive.*

Right: The view down the platforms with an express stationed on the mixed gauge tracks. Each baseboard of Acton was 12ft long making them heavy to move. *Pete Waterman Archive.*

Left: Victorian era passengers look on as the *Ocean Mails* passes through Acton. *Pete Waterman Archive.*

Right: A '633' 0-6-0T passes underneath the road level station building on the mixed gauge track at Acton. *Pete Waterman Archive.*

With a mixed parcels and passenger working behind a '633' 0-6-0T enters the station illustrating the mixed broad and standard gauge track between the platforms. *Pete Waterman Archive.*

Change of tack

With a booming music career, time for modelling changed and while it never left Pete's mind new scales took his attention. **PETE WATERMAN** reveals how and why he started collecting unique and special 'O' gauge and Gauge One locomotives.

As my music career really took off, I changed tack as I didn't have the time available to spend on modelling that I really wanted to, so instead I decided to collect locomotives for display in my office on Hyde Park Corner in London. But 4mm didn't really work when it came to making an impact, and that was what I really wanted, so I switched to 'O' gauge and Gauge One (7mm:1ft and 10mm:1ft scales).

I remember buying my first Gauge One locomotive - a GWR 'Queen' class 2-2-2. I loved it. Then I bought a GWR 'River' class 2-4-0. But there wasn't much else around that I liked or wanted, so I went in search of builders who could create what I was after.

When I'd been in the Midlands, I used to drop into Bearwood Models in Birmingham. They were more into the larger scales which suited my new direction. I've never really been interested in Bing or Bassett-Lowke models,

GWR Churchward 'Saint' 2920 *Saint David* was amongst the first Gauge One locomotives to be built for Pete Waterman by George McKinnon-Ure. Every single part was cast or cut by hand to create the ultimate in detail at 10mm:1ft scale. It was painted by Alan Brackenborough. *Mike Wild.*

but one week I met George McKinnon-Ure. He had an 'O' gauge Caledonian 0-6-0, and it was stunning. After a long conversation, he invited me to his home, and after some time, I knew he was the builder for me.

We struck a deal, and George started to build some 10mm:1ft GWR Gauge One locomotives for me. I could see straight away that he was the best builder I had ever met. He was so low-key about his skills.

I set him a challenge: build the best locomotives he could from scratch, without using anyone else's parts. He was to make all the patterns himself and make no compromises to make the absolute best scale models humanly possible. I gave him all the time he needed to make them as perfect as possible, there was never a deadline, just a requirement for quality.

QUALITY FIRST

He started with a 'Saint' and a 'Lady' 4-6-0. To begin building the locomotives he made all the patterns and had them cast in lost wax by Slaters. Then he cut all the bodywork from sheet brass. The castings and patterns alone took the best part of a year to create, and they were spectacular – even before they were put together. He found someone to make wheels to the same standard and began the assembly.

By the end of year two, the results were breathtaking with every single part hand made with pipework, fittings, bolt heads, rivets – everything on the real locomotive – recreated in miniature. Alan Brackenborough painted them and I was over the moon with the results.

Next, George started on a Churchward '28XX' and the later Collett '2884' 2-8-0. We

> *"We raised the bar higher, pushing the boundaries of what was possible in a model locomotive."*
>
> **PETE WATERMAN**

raised the bar even higher, pushing the boundaries of what was possible in a model locomotive. Part of the idea was to show that we still had people in the UK capable of building the very best in the world. It took three years to build each one of these locomotives and they were so special that I decided to leave them unpainted, to showcase his workmanship in brass and

"They are a testament to a skilled man, left to do what he did best without compromise."

PETE WATERMAN

copper. They are a testament to a skilled man, left to do what he did best without compromise.

George wasn't a young man when we started, and time was running out. He worked on two more 'O' gauge locomotives for me, but sadly, his time was up. What he built was absolutely first class and being able to sit back and admire those metal models of the GWR 2-8-0s is something to savour.

'SUPER D'

There is another Gauge One locomotive that I'm particularly proud of – my 'Super D' 0-8-0. Now, I've always had a soft spot for these LNWR freight locomotives having seen them countless times at Leamington Spa and Rugby in their final years. It's also well known that I funded the restoration of the last surviving 'Super D' – 49395 from the National Collection – which saw that locomotive return to steam after a colossal overhaul at LNWR's Crewe Works in 2005. It continued to operate until being retired in January 2014 at the East Lancashire Railway. It has since been on static display again.

In Gauge One I wanted a 10mm:1ft 'Super D' to replicate the real locomotives not just in its accuracy but also its paint finish. The model was scratchbuilt by Geoff Holt in the 1970s – Geoff being one of the premiere model builders of the period. It was fully detailed, motored and operational and was part of a plan to build a complete working railway in Gauge One.

Having received the completed model and numbering it as Rugby's (2A) 49245, it was crying out to be given a weathered finish, but at the time that wasn't what you did. Brian Caldicott carried out the weathering around 35-40 years ago. No one was weathering locomotives like this back then, nobody. That was because everyone thought of Gauge One models as collectors items, no one saw them as models to work a railway with. If you made any change to how they were delivered the perception was that they would be worth nothing.

This 'Super D' was totally scratchbuilt – there was nothing around at that time in terms of kits – and it was built to 10mm:1ft rather than the 3/8in:1ft scale used by the live steam Gauge One modellers.

There was always a plan to build a Gauge One layout, but when I started to measure it out the shock hit me as to how big it would have to be and how big of a task it would be to actually build. It became obvious very quickly that it wasn't a goer and was something that I could never achieve. I'd got some 'O' gauge models already and very soon realised that if I wanted the detail that was the way to go. ■

George McKinnon-Ure's hand-built GWR 2-8-0s featuring unique castings, copper pipework and hand cut brass sheet for the main structure. The detail is out of this world. *Mike Wild.*

A pair of GWR 2-8-0s modelling the Churchward '28XX' and Collett '2884' designs were commissioned from George McKinnon-Ure with the pair taking three years to complete. Pete kept them in original unpainted brass to showcase their detail. *Mike Wild.*

This 'Super D' was built for a planned Gauge One layout. It was built from scratch by Geoff Holt and weathered by Brian Caldicott to represent Rugby's 49245. *Mike Wild.*

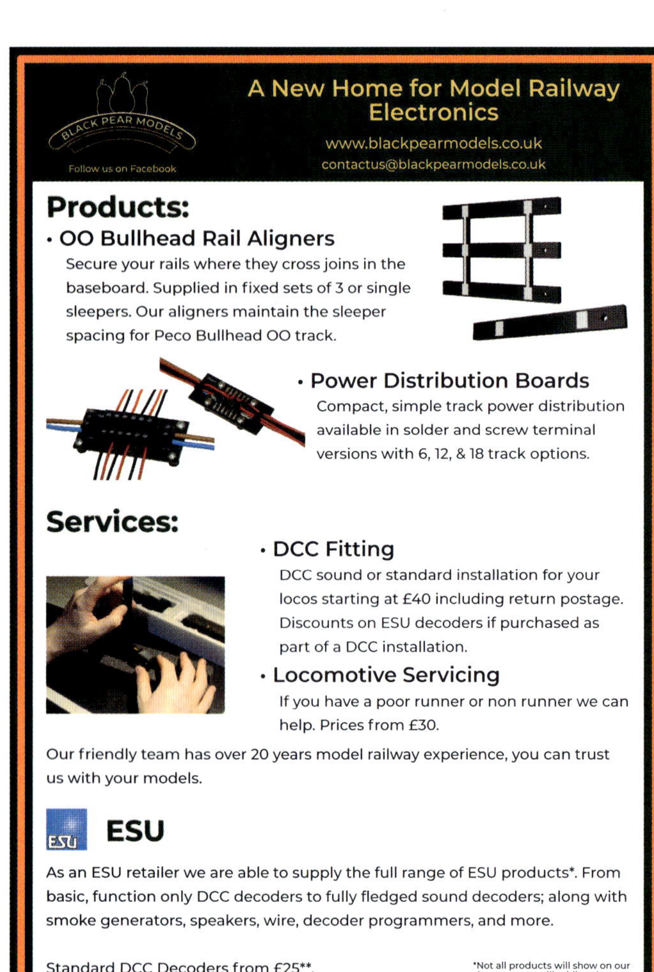

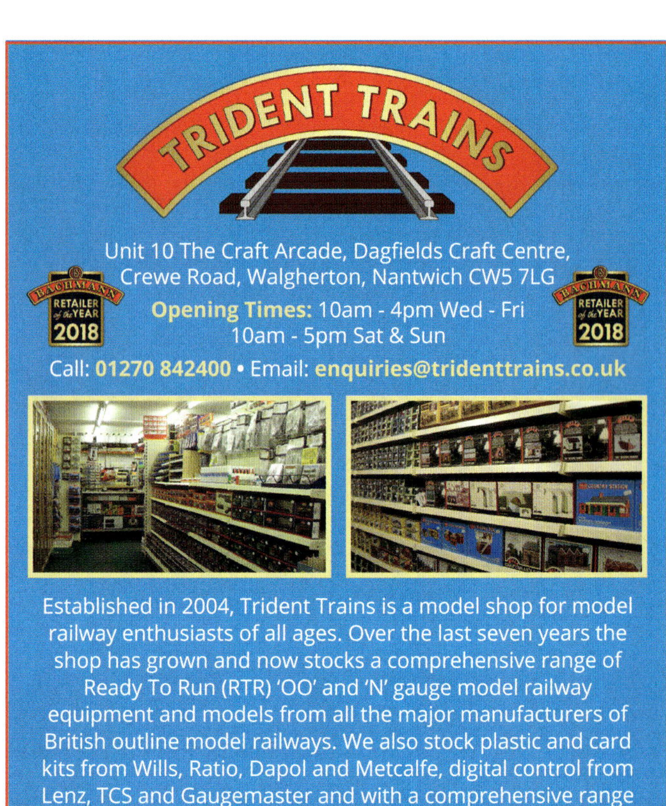

DCCconcepts
CAB
ACC
Cobalt α Central

thinking outside the square
DCC concepts

LOCOMOTION MODELS

Entering preservation

I was always visiting preserved railways as soon as they started in the 1970s, and it was always my intention to get a locomotive to be part of the movement. I had visited Barry, but I was not in the right place at the right time and was not part of any group trying to buy a steam locomotive. I was also more interested in diesels, as there seemed less interest in them at that time.

It was a visit to the East Lancashire Railway (ELR) in its very early days that started the ball rolling. The volunteers there were a great bunch and very keen to build a railway, and only 20 minutes from my home. Back then the railway had a short siding from the Bury Museum yard which it occupied from 1972, but with the impending closure of the line by BR it had big plans. The group had just restored a Class 24 and said they would like a Class 25, and that's how it all started.

I was very green about how to go about becoming a locomotive owner, but the group explained the BR tender procedure and how it worked. I found it impossible to work out. Handily I was doing a Radio 4 programme and one of the guests was British Railways Chairman Peter Parker, so I asked him for some advice. He put me on to his office, which asked Derby to send me a tender document. I was invited to talk to the guys at Derby to tell them what I wanted, as at that time the main people bidding for diesel locomotives were scrap dealers. I explained I wanted a Class 25 for the ELR, so they said they would put me on the list.

A couple of weeks later I had a call to say that Derby had a Class 25 that BR wanted preserved, as they had offered it to another party and they had turned it down. I still had to tender, but as it was to go to Bury, they told me the locomotive weight and the price of scrap per tonne. They then added that if I was successful and would allow the locomotive to go to the Coalville open day, they would deliver it to Bury. 25909, originally D7659, was the last locomotive ever built in Manchester and the last diesel delivered in two-tone green which for me sealed its right to be saved for preservation.

DREAM COME TRUE

Being involved with the ELR was fantastic for me, as they had so many ideas, and to say they were driven is an understatement. I worked with them to make their dream come

Modelling was all about capturing realism in miniature, but when **PETE WATERMAN** had the opportunity to own full size locomotives in preservation he jumped at the chance, leading to a long-standing association with railway heritage including operating the first main line registered preserved diesel locomotive and restoring one of the unsung heroes of freight by rail. He explains how it all started.

Class 25 D7659 was the last locomotive to built in Manchester and the last to be completed in BR two-tone green when it entered traffic in 1966. More recently it has been based at Peak Rail where it is in operational condition and managed by the Waterman Heritage Trust. On August 13 2022 it arrives at Darley Dale heading to Rowsley South. *Tom McAtee/Alamy Stock Photo.*

The first main line registered heritage diesel was Pete Waterman's Class 46 D172 *Ixion*. It departs Crewe heading Pathfinder Railtours 'North Wales Coast Explorer' from Swindon to Holyhead on August 26 1996 alongside Class 37/4 37417. *John Whitehouse.*

true. There seemed nothing they could not do. I was buying stock that they wanted – BR Mk 1s and Mk 2s, a few wagons, and an inspection saloon and became the President.

They were the first to hold a diesel gala. It did cause a bit of a stir. It seems strange now looking back to see the fight we had to do it, though diesel preservation was still in its infancy back then, but I agreed to underwrite any loss. It was an amazing weekend, beating all the other events that year. Soon, other railways followed, and we were invited to take our locomotives out to other events as the interest in diesel traction began to grow. The next year I took one of my electrics and we operated it being dragged by the diesels. We were having great fun and bringing in good funds for the ELR at the same time. Suffice to say, diesel galas became an integral part of annual planning on heritage railways.

However, there was a downside – 25mph. While this was quite right to have a speed restriction on a heritage railway, there was a group of diesel owners who wanted to run them on the main line, but there was a ban on ex-BR diesel locomotives being operated on the national network.

We were invited to a meeting of SLOA – the Steam Locomotive Operator's Association. They invited us to join as junior members. A couple of us were a bit more up for it than that, so we talked to BR ourselves. We found the door could be opened, maybe, if we had a diesel with two engines. That meant a 'Deltic' or a 'Western'. The thinking was that if one engine went down, they could still get by on the other engine. I had D1048 *Western Lady*, but the work needed was out of the question.

Then I saw an opening - *Ixion*, a Class 46, came up for sale. *Ixion* had started life as D172 and later became 46035 when the TOPS numbering system came in. However, it

had really gained its fame by becoming part of the Railway Technical Centre (RTC) fleet where it was number 97403 and carried the red and blue colour scheme of the RTC. It had been used for adhesion tests and was finally withdrawn and put on the tender list in 1990 – the last Class 46 to become available.

I went to see it at Derby. It had been used up to a couple of weeks before by the RTC, and though it had been modified for use in railway testing, it was a better option as we could do most of the work ourselves at Crewe.

The Class 46 is really a Class 47 in the body of a Class 45. I knew that it would not be easy, so I contracted the major work out to Crewe Diesel Depot - that was the home of Rail Express Systems Crewe which had a fleet of Class 47s, 86s and 90s. We would do all the bodywork and painting, and they would do the bogies and engine together with the certification. This got round lots of the problems we were about to have with BR.

To give you some context its now 1994 right at the start of privatisation and at this point there are still no heritage diesel locomotives registered to work on the main line. Finding out what had to be done to get *Ixion* main line registered was a challenge. No one really wanted to make a decision, and there wasn't a structure in place. We had to accept this, and I had sort of worked it out, but with the Crewe contact in place, I had an ace.

A set of criteria was given to us that we would have to meet before we were allowed to run on the main line. Two engines only - foul. At that point I knew they had not thought it through. "OK then," I said "you have to stop all your diesel engines."

Now the look of horror, the intake of air, was a shock. "Why?" was the question? "Well," I replied, "my 46 is a 47 all but in body, and being maintained by BR at Crewe alongside

the Rail Express Systems (RES) Class 47s - so why is mine different?" Blank looks.

They had to make a phone call, and so did I. I called the man in charge at RES Crewe, who was shocked at what I told him. The question I should ask them, he said, was: how would he get the RES Class 47s home without an engine? The answer was simply that he would send another locomotive to recover it, so why could he not do the same for us?

I could see now that privatisation was going to present big challenges to the heritage movement. The government had set up a vendor unit to sell BR off. It sounded easy, but it would cause massive upheaval to the railway. The main point in the beginning was to set up Train Operating Companies (TOCs), Rolling Stock Companies (ROSCO) and Railtrack – the infrastructure manager. No TOC was to own any stock; it would be leased from the ROSCOs, and all infrastructure was owned by Railtrack. There was to be open access, and a fee paid per mile. The government did not want to sell the freight operation, and there was to be no Special Train Unit.

FLYING SCOTSMAN

A year earlier in 1993 I bought a 50% stake in *Flying Scotsman*. The truth is that I never wanted to own it, as I was never an LNER man – I was always a Great Western man. However, I could see that Bill McAlpine was in financial trouble because of the Gresley 'A3' and I felt that what he had done for railway preservation needed supporting.

Once we had done the deal, we had some fun together. Bill was the most wonderful human being and he had such a huge impact on preservation. I had started working on getting preserved diesel traction back on the main line, but Bill asked if I had considered owning a steam locomotive.

On September 11 2024 Freightliner Class 90 90041 was named *Pete Waterman OBE RBF* at Crewe station. The naming was kept completely secret to make it a surprise at the unveiling. The naming recognises Pete's connection as President of the Railway Benefit Fund. *John Whitehouse.*

> *"It blew me away. I've spent years taking names at the lineside - and then wait a minute, there's my name on a 90. I'd never considered it."*
>
> **PETE WATERMAN**

I met him at the Gloucestershire Warwickshire Railway and Bill and I rode up and down with him extolling the virtues of 60103. Next week it was moving to Bury at the East Lancashire Railway and I was gobsmacked by the reaction to it – people were even buying lumps of coal from it and that's when I realised there was something about this locomotive.

We got a deal in place where I took over Flying Scotsman Enterprises, but I soon saw that all wasn't as it seemed. The trains weren't making any money and I said to Bill that we needed to do things differently and treat operating *Flying Scotsman* like a proper business. This led to us bringing in a professional approach to railway preservation, creating apprenticeships to build new skills for people and keep old skills alive.

SPECIAL TRAINS
Interlinked with *Flying Scotsman* and *Ixion* was the opportunity to take on the Special Trains Unit from British Rail at the start of privatisation. I had a meeting with Chris Green, Head of InterCity, and put forward the case for the Special Train Unit. He went to the BR Board and a meeting was set up with the vendor unit. We started a round of meetings that went on for some time. They agreed to put the Special Trains Unit up for sale as long as it was understood there would be no subsidies and it could not run scheduled trains. I then pointed out that if we didn't own the assets, we would have nothing to run with. We were told we would have to lease them! From who? The ROSCOs? Why would they want stock that was old, used very little, and vacuum braked?

After many meetings it was agreed that the sale of the Special Train Unit would include its assets which meant we had the rolling stock needed to operate the charters. Now

we had to find an affiliate TOC that could supply drivers and a safety case which would also look after the maintenance. RES was the perfect fit once again and we now had a TOC and had to start understanding how the charges for the track would work.

It was still 1994 and the privatisation of the railways was still in its early stages, so everything was a learning curve. Railtrack hadn't even been set up, so who was to give a price? And how could you bid for something when you had no idea what it would cost? Everybody connected went into a huddle.

We had won the tender for the Special Trains Unit - and that's when it went wrong. The good news was that the first year you were a shadow franchise, meaning it was still run by BR. The sale had included six Class 47s and around 200 carriages from the Mk 1, Mk 2 and Mk 3 fleets, but there was a lot to untangle to operate the business successfully.

At the time, we were based at Paddington, so I started a weekly meeting with the staff of the Special Trains Unit and the staff of Flying Scotsman Enterprises (FSE) which I brought together. The first thing to understand was who were our clients, other than SLOA for steam tours. There were three luxury trains - two private and one operated by BR which was the Luxury Land Cruise. The Land Cruise was operated by Special Trains while the other two private trains were run by Flying Scotsman Enterprises. The Land Cruise went out from London on a Friday after lunch and back Monday late afternoon. One week it went to Oban, and the next to Kyle of Lochalsh.

The train had sleeping coaches, kitchen and dining cars, all in InterCity livery with white roofs. It ran from Easter to September. It was always sold out and, if I remember right, had 65 passengers. The traction was a Class 90 to Scotland, then two Class 37s, and

back down the East Coast Main Line with the Class 90. I soon discovered that it had been running at a loss on every trip. The food bill alone was fantastic – the food was fantastic too – and the losses were eye-watering. There was no way this could carry on under private ownership and in the end the Scottish Weekend working would never run again as at best we were breaking even.

MAINTENANCE
Having experienced the change of the railway and the cost involved in working with the BR Works, I decided to look into the maintenance side of the railway – something I was far more comfortable with. My first steam locomotive needed a ten-year overhaul, so having considered all the options we decided to do it ourselves.

I had read the book on group standards - that were to be the way the railway would run in the future - and could see that the engineering side would become more important than ever. We set up ISO 9002 - a first in the rail industry which set the standards for quality management around installation and servicing, and this helped hugely with gaining contracts.

One of those contracts came through FSE which had been given the job of building the train for the Disney film *The Hunchback of Notre Dame*. The railway wanted this train to prove it was open for business, but the task was huge. It was to be a travelling exhibition and the job of ripping the interiors out, refitting, changing windows and doors, and air-braking was one thing - getting it past group standards was another. In the time we had, it seemed impossible, but this was to be different.

Railtrack called a meeting with all involved and said it had to happen. For me it was the first time I'd seen the attitude: "We *can* do this." It was unbelievable. We got the train out on time, all complete and Disney were delighted. This led to more work on coaches for VSOE and so it built up.

Soon after, I had a call to visit Railtrack after a board meeting, as they were in the same building. They wanted change and had been impressed by the way we had got everybody working together on the Disney job. They wanted to have an independent company in the maintenance business. Would we take on Crewe Carriage Shed on a peppercorn rent and build it up?

Of course the answer was yes and we built a great business looking after Class 66s, 86s and 90s for Freightliner and the Virgin Voyager fleet. The shed wasn't being used and we spent over £7 million to install new

The sole-surviving LNWR 'Super D' 0-8-0 was returned to working order by Pete Waterman at LNWR Crewe. On January 22 2007 the immaculate 0-8-0 leads the 'Windcutter' 16ton mineral wagon train on the approach to Quork on the Great Central Railway. *Mike Wild*.

equipment including a wheel lathe, retention toilet waste emptying systems and we even added special telemetry equipment so that we could look after the tilting Super Voyagers for Virgin Trains.

Then we gained the contract for Heavy Haul which saw us build the facility at Leeds Balm Road (often referred to as Leeds Midland Road Depot) and we were the first to replace pits with rails on the supports like in Europe – we visited sites in Italy and France to discover how it could be done.

Both of these were huge installations as part of that business to meet the needs of maintaining modern trains, but it was a fantastic time which I thoroughly enjoyed every minute of. This was the dream of that boy who stood on Leamington Spa station back in the 1950s – owning his own railway facility and looking after the maintenance of locomotives and rolling stock.

STEAM ENGINEERING

The steam side was amazing - with boilers as far as the eye could see – as the LNWR Crewe Works at the Crewe Heritage Centre built up its client base and reputation for quality standards. It took care of the restoration of the National Collection's LNWR 'Super D' 0-8-0 49395 which I was immensely proud to see brought back to working order.

It was a homage to my youth and train spotting days. 'Super Ds' were a major feature of the railway line next to my school and I'd watch six trains a day go past the window and at least four of those would have 'Super Ds' on the front. They were important to me and I was always fascinated with them.

I'd seen 49395 when it was at Leicester Tram Museum in its early years of preservation. It later went to the museum

at Ironbridge Gorge Museum and when the railway business was starting to motor really well and I had a thought: I'm not interested in *Flying Scotsman*. What if I offered the National Railway Museum the money to bring the 'Super D' back into working order?

What we didn't understand back then was the difference between what a museum sees as a restoration and what we would do to bring it back into working order. The museum wanted to restore it under contract, but it was costing so much to restore, so I took it into LNWR Crewe and brought two of the last Premium Apprentices from Crewe to work on the locomotive and to advise on how to move it forward. One of them was the last guy to set valves on 'Super Ds' at Crewe – he was

absolutely immersed in these locomotives and showed how little we knew about them. At that point the project took on a whole new life.

It had last steamed in around 1955 and it had survived by being hidden at Buxton because it was a favourite of the foreman's there. It was 50 years old in preservation even before we touched it! It had all sorts of strange things like brass bottle ends on the end of tubes.

We finally got it back in steam and it was a great day! We then took it down to the Churnet Valley Railway and got it run in, but it had to be treated differently. It was completely different to anything else. The crews had to be on their wits all the time, otherwise it would catch them out. The fire

Pete Waterman at the unveiling of HS2's 2,000 tonne tunnel boring machine on October 20 2021 that has created a one-mile twin bore tunnel under Long Itchington Wood, Warwickshire. The machine has been named *Dorothy*, after Dorothy Hodgkin the first British woman to win the Nobel Prize in Chemistry, following a public vote. *PA Images/Alamy Stock Photo*.

Pete Waterman stands on the buffer of Class 45 D120 in the company of Class 47 D1501 and Class 81 E3003 in the mid-1990s. *Roger Bamber/Alamy Stock Photo.*

had to be white hot all the time, you couldn't just fill it with coal, and the drivers had to be so careful of carry over into the cylinders.

It was the sound of the 'Super D' that was so unusual – they sounded so strange, but that was how they were. It went down to Minehead in 2008 for the West Somerset Railway gala and coming up the bank to Washford it sounded fantastic – that was one of the greatest days of my life. It just walked up those hills as if they weren't there. The sun was shining, we were sweating like crazy, but we loved it. I went to bed that night at peace with the world.

I now had four of my own steam engines – GWR 'Prairie' 2-6-2T 5553, '5205' 2-8-0T 5224, '56XX' 0-6-2T 6634 and 'Castle' 4-6-0 7027 *Thornbury Castle* - but never seemed to have the time to get on them back then. Today 5553 is operational at Peak Rail while the 2-8-0T is being overhauled and the 0-6-2T is waiting for its turn. These three locomotives are owned by the Waterman Heritage Trust together with my first ever diesel D7659, *Ixion* and my Class 47 47402 which are also at Peak Rail.

SUPPORTING THE FUTURE

While I owned LNWR Crewe I worked with the Labour Government on the Future Jobs Fund to reintroduce apprenticeships which saw us create skilled workers in boiler and railway locomotive maintenance and I was also appointed to the Cheshire and Warrington LEP as Deputy Chair of Transport, later to be Chair

and was appointed as a Director of Transport for the North and this even included being responsible for getting High Speed 2 (HS2) north of Birmingham to reach Crewe.

I started on the railway in 1962 as a shed boy at Stafford Road, Wolverhampton and now I was one of the first directors of Transport for the North.

There have been lots of ups and downs in my career with the railway, but I had never lost the love for the railway and its workers who are the best friends I've had for over 50 years. I'm President of the Railway Benefit Fund which provides support to current, former and retired railway people and their families across the UK.

I joined as a Patron around six years ago to raise money for the RBF and its been one of the best things I've done in my life to be involved with it. Not everybody is a driver and many of the railway staff can't afford to live on their wages. So we are out here trying to make a difference.

When I joined the RBF there was a call for its help every 20 minutes, now it's a call every four minutes. Part of that is that we go out and campaign. We are out there talking to people on the trains and on the platforms to get people to help raise money for the RBF and to make railway workers aware of the RBF. What railway people do for the public is staggering and often not seen.

It's an incredibly important charity which does brilliant work to support people from

the railway at all levels. I was both surprised and honoured to unveil the naming of Class 90 90041 *Pete Waterman OBE RBF* at Crewe station on September 11 2024. It was totally unexpected, I'd gone along to unveil a new name on a Class 90, but I had no idea that Freightliner's CEO Tim Shoveller was making an introduction to my own locomotive naming.

The naming blew me away! You have to remember I'm a trainspotter and I've spent years taking names at the lineside like great engineers and Kings – and then wait a minute, there's my name on a Class 90! I'd never considered it. They don't normally name locomotives unless you work on the railway, so it really caught me by surprise.

The world has changed dramatically on the railway since I started commuting from London to Coventry in 1971, but I've enjoyed every minute of it. I've commuted on the West Coast Main Line every week for 55 years and in that time I've seen it change, but I still look out the window and watch the seasons and the world around move with the times. Houses appear where once it was open fields. Children sometimes still wave at the train, as I did back in the early 1950s.

That's the magic of trains - you only get a fleeting glimpse. You never will meet the people on that train, but for that brief second, you're one. What a journey. What a life. If only my granddad could see what he started. Wow. ■

Electric connection

From the first moment **PETE WATERMAN** saw one of the new West Coast AC electrics at the turn of the '60s, he was hooked which led him to preserve as many as possible of the original locomotive types. Pete explains how he came to save the AC electrics and how it has impacted his modelling.

The West Coast electrics have been a passion for Pete Waterman since his first sight of one at Rugby at the turns of the 1960s. On Making Tracks 5, a pair of Freightliner Class 86s roar along the slow lines on the approach to Bushey as a Class 390 overtakes. *Mike Wild.*

They thought I was mad to want to preserve electric locomotives, but to me these were special locomotives which had a rightful place in the history of British Railways.

Right from the first time I saw one of the new AC electrics tucked away inside Rugby's Mill Street Works I was fascinated by this new form of traction. At their introduction I heard from a couple of lads on Rugby station that they had seen the first of them moved through the station. I guessed that they had been stored in the old railway works in Rugby on Mill Street. I remember creeping round the back with my box brownie and peering in through a broken window to take a picture to prove it.

I remember taking that picture, and it was a box brownie so it was the worst picture ever, but it was such a moment, it was like seeing spaceships. It was so fantastic to see that electric blue with white cab roofs and stainless steel lettering in a works which had been used to maintain 'Super Ds' under the London North Western Railway. It showed a new age of rail travel was here.

Back then at the end of the 1950s and into the 1960s Rugby was a massive site for railways. As a kid Rugby was enormous and it was packed full of locomotives and with the testing plant close to the station there was often something new or different in the area.

The new electrics though were totally different to the steam locomotives, and even the early diesels on the West Coast Main Line. Where we had previously had a diet of BR maroon Stanier 'Pacifics' and dark green English Electric Type 4s on the fastest expresses, all of a sudden there was a reminder of that first sighting of the prototype 'Deltic' back at Brinklow with the electric blue livery of the new order.

The original AC electrics were rugged simple locomotives, nothing like the modern electric locomotives you see on the main line railway today. There were five main types introduced for the first phase of electrification on the West Coast Main Line: the Class 81 from AEI/BRCW (originally designed by British Thomson-Houston), the Class 82 from Metropolitan-Vickers/Beyer, Peacock, the Class 83 from English Electric, the Class 84 from North British and the Class 85 from British Railways own Works at Doncaster.

These prototype classes were built to assess the performance of the new AC electrics and later lead to construction of the Class 86 which was the largest single class of AC electric locomotive to be built for the British railway network with 100 being completed between 1965-1966 at Doncaster Works and English Electric's Vulcan Foundry.

> *"It was so fantastic to see the electric blue and white cab roofs and stainless steel lettering. It showed a new age of rail travel."*
>
> **PETE WATERMAN**

The Doncaster Works built Class 85s were amongst Pete's favourite WCML locomotives and lead to him preserve 85101. On January 22 1978 85007 pauses at Crewe with a cross country service from Liverpool. *John Chalcraft/Railphotoprints.uk.*

The original Class 81-85, first known as AL1-AL5, arrived from 1959 with the first on the scene being the Class 81s. These locomotives were the forerunners of main line electrification at 25kV AC on the British network which set the standard for all future electrification programmes. Previously we had seen the 1,500V DC supply installed on the Woodhead Route, but the heavy cost of this system combined with the need for more substations to power it saw the 25kV AC system adopted.

I always thought the Class 76s and 77s on the 1,500V DC Woodhead route were amazing, but I only really saw them in the latter days. I was lucky enough to travel behind the 76s and watch the coal traffic. By that time I was travelling and delivering records to radio stations and I was always looking to be close to a railway at lunchtime.

I love the pantographs on the Class 76s as well as the catenary and their noise was so different to the AC electrics drawing from the 1,500V DC. I guess again it was a freight railway which drew me and if I was in the Pennine area I'd always find a way to stop and see them.

The Woodhead route didn't last much longer as it was closed for good in 1981 and by this time the first of the West Coast AC electrics were also being withdrawn. In fact, some of the first Class 81-85 series locomotives were stood down as early as 1968 though others had a longer career with the last – a Class 85 – being stood down in 1992.

The Class 83 was one of the final two of the original WCML electric classes to be saved for preservation. 83012 was the locomotive selected, as it had been retained for empty stock movements between Wembley and Euston. On September 14 1982 83012 heads a lengthy northbound passenger service through Stafford. *Brian Robbins/Railphotoprints.uk.*

PRESERVATION

The story of my preservation of the first generation of electrics began with the regret that there had not been a Fowler 'Patriot' 4-6-0 preserved. I always liked the 'Patriots', and they had a great reputation with the men who used them - most would have had one over a 'Royal Scot' as they were better engines which steamed more freely and were suited to the work they did.

The 'Patriots' were a nod back to the LNWR whereas the 'Scots' were pure LMS. Those who remembered working on the LNWR locomotives felt at home with the 'Patriot'. It was similar with the AC electrics – they were hard working locomotives, but few saw the value back then in preserving electrics at all.

I had already started to preserve diesel locomotives in the mid-1980s with a Class 25 and 45 in my collection. The problem I saw was that diesels could be used on the East Lancashire Railway, or any other heritage railway for that matter, but an electric? Where could one of those run, would it even be possible for them to run again?

At that moment, Crewe Heritage Centre needed help, so I became Chair of the Trust. They had very little running line, so in effect, they were a museum located between the West Coast Main Line to the east of the site and the line to Chester on the west forming a triangular site. They already had the Advanced Passenger Train, so it seemed that the first generation of AC electrics would fit the collection, as well being right next to the route they served. Interestingly, this outlook continues today as Crewe Heritage Centre is home to examples of the Class 87, 90, 91 and 370 APT all on display.

Back in the late 1980s the way you bought from BR was by tender. You put in a bid and waited to see if you had been successful. At this time, the tender lists were long, and there was always temptation to look at a diesel that could be used instead. Looking back, I was pretty determined to save one of each of the first generation of electrics so that future generations could see what changed - the way life changed with their introduction, as their impact was huge.

It was the introduction of the one-hour-twenty train service from Birmingham to Euston that meant Coventry was one hour from London. That couldn't be done before

The Class 86s were the largest single AC electric class to be built. On May 31 1985 86223 *Hector* enters at Stockport with the Down Manchester Pullman. *Alan H Bryant ARPS/Railphotoprints.uk.*

The Metropolitan Vickers/Beyer, Peacock Class 82s were a small class of ten locomotives with the last being withdrawn in 1987. 82005 stands at London Euston with a Royal Mail TPO from Stonebridge Park on October 25 1983. *Gordon Edgar/Railphotoprints.uk.*

thought that told the story better to be able to illustrate the full story of the first five main line electrics from the WCML.

The Class 85s were still in service as they were the last of the early breeds to be withdrawn, so perhaps, just perhaps, I thought one could be used for specials. The story at this point takes on a life of its own. All the AL1s to AL5s had asbestos in them, so this had to be removed before they could be sold other than for scrap. That was a problem. It meant that BR had no choice but to sell them to the scrap man, because the asbestos had to be removed before they could be scrapped, and a certificate sent to BR to prove it. So how could I get around this problem?

Derby came up with the answer. They would sell it to the scrap man, he would remove the asbestos, then when they had the document, they could sell it to me as scrap. It seemed like a way around it, but that would be too easy, and now it got complicated, and I mean complicated!

Because the asbestos had to be removed by a licensed dealer, most of the electrics ended up in Glasgow at Jim McWilliams, where he had a shop that removed asbestos, and he was a scrap dealer that worked for BR. So, I would buy the locomotives from Jim? Easy? No. He was not allowed to resell them as locomotives. After lots of phone calls, letters, and a meeting in Derby, Jim was given permission to sell them to me with the written approval of BR.

Although an expensive way of doing things, it was the only way. It meant a lorry from Crewe to Glasgow, and a lorry back to Crewe. I then decided to have them repainted and put back together in Heysham, so Glasgow to Heysham and then to Crewe. So now it's three lorries, more cost.

The Class 82s and 83s were all on the tender lists, but most had been fire damaged, so were beyond saving. But Jim had one 82 that was fine, so the deal was done and that saw 82008 saved for the future alongside Class 81 81002 and Class 84 84001. This left the AL3 and AL5 to sort, and here it got really interesting. The

the introduction of electric traction, it simply wasn't possible. This increase in speed had a personal connection too as it meant I could travel to and from London easily and still live in Coventry and keep on DJing. I felt that without these first electrics, I would not have been so successful.

By the time I was looking to preserve the WCML electrics, I was no longer living in Coventry. I'd moved to Warrington, so the electrics meant even more to me - under two hours from home to central London! The NRM had already preserved a Class 84, so that was one off the list. There was also a Class 81 at the Heritage Centre that I was told was up for sale. So, with the AL1 and AL4 safe, I needed an AL2 and AL3. But, and it was a big but, I wanted to add an AL5, as I

The new West Coast electrics of the early 1960s were unlike anything which had gone before on the route with their electric blue livery, white cab roofs and stainless steel numbers and crests. Carrying its original livery, AL5 E3020 (later Class 85 85017) powers through Acton Bridge in May 1965. *Colin Whitfield/Railphotoprints.uk.*

word was out on what I was doing, and to some it seemed heresy.

It sounds crazy, but what was about to unfold was, and still is, amazing. The fact that I had said that if I could, I would like the Class 85 to run on specials brought out significant opposition. At the time, I had no idea of this, because no one had thought of preserved electrics as heritage traction. I had people in BR who were going out of their way to help, they were railwaymen who understood what I was trying to do, but there were others that weren't so keen on the idea.

It's fair to say that preserving diesels was weird to some back then, so electrics must have seemed crazy to most. But some got it. While it was okay to go to scrapyards in South Wales and buy the remains of steam engines, diesels on the other hand - were we mad? Who wanted these smelly things?

At this point there was one Class 83, 83012, still left in traffic at Wembley for empty carriage movements to and from Euston, and it was about to be withdrawn. Did I want it? Boy, did I. So it went to Jim's in Glasgow for stripping and became part of the collection which left me with one more for the goal to be completed.

COMPLETING THE SET

As mad as it may seem, I was shocked by some of the resistance I met. I understood the main concern, but it was not my view. By then, there were very few of the first generation of AC electrics left, let alone working, and some were keen for there to be none.

I persevered, and at last, we had all the first generation saved with 85101 (original 85006) joining the collection at Crewe Heritage Centre. Sadly they would not be able to run again, but they were there to see, and for

Pete's interest in electric traction didn't stop with the original designs. A BR Class 90 leads a container train on Making Tracks 2 recreating the mid-2000s on the WCML. *Mike Wild.*

generations to see how crude they were but also to learn about the impact they had on people's lives. I can't imagine being able to do what I did in the music industry if it wasn't for the speed of the West Coast electrics.

All five remain today with the Class 81, 82, 83 and 85 all located at Barrow Hill Roundhouse under the ownership of the AC Locomotive Group which has cared for them since 1997 while 84001 is on display at the National Railway Museum's York museum. Since then

these pioneers of electric traction on the West Coast have been seen at depot open days at Crewe, Toton, Old Oak Common and Doncaster with their next public outing set to be at The Greatest Gathering on August 1-3 2025 at Alstom's Derby Litchurch Lane Works.

There was another locomotive that I bid for – the Class 89. The unique 1986 Brush Traction designed Class 89 was put up for silent bid and I won the bid to buy it. However, I then heard from BR that it had

On Making Tracks 2 a Hornby Class 87 recreates the early privatisation years with a rake of Virgin Trains liveried Mk 3s. Modelling the WCML in 'OO' gauge was made simple with ready-to-run AC electrics. *Mike Wild.*

Prior to starting Making Tracks Pete had a series of 'O' gauge models built by Dave Lowery from etched kits. This is Class 86 86608 *St John Ambulance* in Railfreight Distribution livery. *Mike Wild.*

The BR blue Class 85s were among Pete's favourites of the originl designs. This etched brass kit has been finished as 85014 with a weathered finish. *Mike Wild.*

been withdrawn from tender as Brush was taking it back, after which it was returned to service with GNER and enjoyed a career on the main line between 1997 and 2000 mainly working the London King's Cross-Leeds/Bradford turns. Happily, even though it was withdrawn due to a major failure, it is now being returned to working order in a partnership between the AC Locomotive Group and Locomotive Services Limited, so I hope once again to be able to see the Class 89 on the main line in the near future.

ELECTRIC APPEAL

It wasn't just these first five classes that I had such a soft spot for, it was the entire electric fleet. The Woodhead electrics were always a draw, but the West Coast is where I spent most of my time with electric locomotives as I travelled with them three or four times a week – and still do today on the Pendolinos.

The Class 85s were always my favourites. To me they were the first time the AC electrics had been done right, and they laid the foundations for the 86s and 87s. I had mates that drove 85s so I had lots of trips in the cab,

but equally they were never treated with the same reverence as the 86s. I also think it was the Class 85's connection with freight traffic which made them appeal as I have always had a love for freight on the railway.

One of my happiest moments when I was working at LNWR Crewe and looking after the Freightliner fleet was being inundated by all the AC electrics. We had the job of repainting them all and overhauling them and we had all the nameplates too. Freightliner didn't want the names on the locomotives, so we were storing them. It was like being a 14 year all over again but running a business with my own workshop to look after the AC electrics I loved so much. I remember walking into the steam workshop one day and we had the 'Super D' and the 'WD' in there being worked on. And I thought this is my workshop, and in here I've got things that I would have died to have seen as a young trainspotter. Then I could jump in my car, go round to the other site and see Class 86s, 90s, Voyagers all being maintained by the works which was under LNWR Crewe to manage the Freightliner contracts. It was fantastic.

MODELLING THE ELECTRICS

When it came to modelling electrics, I bought all the kits for them in 'O' gauge, but I realised the problem with them was the same as when I wanted the 'Peak' diesels for 'O'. They are very complicated boxes which do not lend themselves to etched metal kits, but that was the technology at that time and that didn't allow you to capture what electrics were because of the shaping. This is where CNC machining and resin mouldings come into play as all those complex shapes can be recreated accurately.

It does sadden me that I wasn't able to do the electrics in 'O' gauge with Just Like the Real Thing, but I have thought about doing them now, even just for myself. I kept the Class 76 etched kits, while the Class 85, 86 and 89 that I have were all built by Dave Lowery using etched metal kits as their basis.

Making Tracks was the first opportunity to model the West Coast Electrics properly for me in a proper model railway scene. The best part was that the models were available off the shelf and the quality is fantastic. For me this was a golden opportunity to make the West Coast easy for me and the boys to model, as we didn't have to touch the stock. When I look at it, I realised I could go to Hornby, Bachmann, Accurascale or Heljan and put that the stock straight on the layout. It saved me upwards of three years of modelling. All I had to do was to create a layout to put these fabulous models on and it also gave me the opportunity to model something else I loved which was scenery in terms of ballast, trees and bushes.

We never had a long time to build each of the Making Tracks layouts, but with the locomotives and stock already done combined with my knowledge of the West Coast we could put all our effort into modelling the railway on which I had spent so much time.

That modern rolling stock was a saviour of Making Tracks. Ultimately though, I'd be more than happy if they were all in 'O' gauge.
• **Read the Making Tracks story on pages 82-89.** ∎

The unique Brush Co-Co electric 89001 *Avocet* has been modelled in 'O' gauge with this etched metal kit. The real locomotive is currently on track to return to the main line with Locomotive Service Limited and the AC Locomotive Group.

Just Like the Real Thing

Just Like the Real Thing was all about detail and creating kits that were designed to be built. The LMS pioneer diesels are amongst the most complex of all with their subtle differences from early testing and modification. A pair of JLTRT kit built models power through Leamington Spa hauling a rake of BR Mk 1 and Stanier 57ft corridor stock. *Mike Wild.*

While working with George McKinnon-Ure on the Gauge One locomotives I had met another incredible builder: Eric Underhill. I'd known Eric for some time, and he stepped into the role to make models for me. Where George had built locomotives for me, Eric's skill was as a pattern maker, and he made the patterns for the Just Like the Real Thing (JLTRT) kits which launched the business in the early 2000s.

The first thing he did was to upgrade the Malcolm Mitchell 7mm finescale kits which I'd bought with lost wax parts for the chassis and the tenders. I'd originally thought I could increase the size of the Mitchell kits to 10mm:1ft scale for the Gauge One layout I'd been considering, but realised that it wasn't going to be feasible and then that's where 'O' gauge took over.

The revitalised Malcolm Mitchell kits were marketed as super-detailing packs, with new backplate parts as well as the underframe and slide bars, and then all the patterns for the new kits. We set up a unit in Bromsgrove to do this; we even did some plastic injection work for the Mk 1 windows. We spent most weekends on field trips at the Severn Valley and other places to gather the photographs and measurements we needed, as well as sampling the local beer!

I had set up JLTRT to get quality into the 'O' gauge market. My first visit to the Telford

Just Like the Real Thing was created to bring 7mm scale modellers top quality, highly detailed kits. **PETE WATERMAN** explains how the company was created and the challenges it faced.

'O' gauge show in 1998 showed how much potential there was in 7mm scale, especially when it came to detail. I also wanted to make kits easier to build without losing the quality as this could draw more modellers into the scale. This meant we had to innovate, something that Eric had done with his own kits. They went together well and had the detail I wanted. Eric had pioneered resin boilers and tanks; they were great value and faster to build than my all metal Mitchell kits,

but just as good. He had sold his kit range before we met, so we had to start fresh.

He had just done the unique Midland Railway 0-10-0 58100 *Big Bertha* – the Lickey Banker. He had been a fireman at Bromsgrove in the 1950s, so that was our first kit together.

The name for the new company was Just Like the Real Thing because that was exactly what our aim was, with a target of producing high-quality finescale 7mm:1ft scale kits and accessories which could be built and

assembled into accurate models of the locomotives and rolling stock we wanted to create.

The plan for Leamington Spa called for rolling stock to model 1947-1960, but at the time all the kits for diesel locomotives were etched metal. This didn't lend itself to the complex shapes of a diesel, so we started to look at a brand-new way of making kits for the scale with diesel locomotives being one of the focuses. The first diesel class we chose was the Class 45 in the early 2000s. The reason was simple, I owned three of them back then – 45041, 45149 and 46035 *Ixion* plus at one time I had 45127 as a source of spares.

The challenge with the diesels was creating accurate castings as they had to be in three parts for the body to allow the correct details of cab and engine room to be modelled. This was a big challenge and required a big investment in both tooling and machinery to make these kits.

The first JLTRT all-new steam locomotive kit was for the Stanier rebuilt 'Royal Scot' 4-6-0 using parts from the real 46115 *Scots Guardsman* for measurements – which was at LNWR Crewe at the time – to make sure we got every single detail just right. The first kit was completed as 46148 *The Manchester Regiment* which I showed on the JLTRT stand at the Manchester Show in the early 2000s.

In the JLTRT workshop Alan Pipkin roughs out a GWR No. 2 boiler and firebox using one of the CNC machine tools. This complex process required skilled modellers. *Pete Waterman.*

The GWR 'King' was amongst the first 'O' gauge kits to be owned by Pete Waterman when he bought the Malcolm Mitchell range in the late 1990s. 6005 *King George II* leads a rake of Bert Collington designed Gresley 61ft 6in corridor stock down Hatton Bank – another signature product of the JLTRT range. *Mike Wild.*

> *"We were on the cutting edge of learning with new materials and methods. Everything before had been etched metal."*

PETE WATERMAN OBE

CUTTING EDGE

We were on a cutting edge of learning with new materials and methods. Everything before had been etched metal which the modeller had to cut and bend and shape, but our way was about to change that. I'd worked out that we needed 150 carriages for Leamington, and there was no way I could build that many etched coaches.

Having seen Bert Collington's original Gresley coaches that he built – I met him around the same time as Eric Underhill, they really impressed me, and I could see that I could build a rake of those in less than two weeks. They were built from resin and he was a clever engineer. He had worked in the shipping industry and had a company making ship alarms for boats and he'd made the Gresley coaches as a sideline under the name Sparmac Models. They were magnificent.

I went up to see Bert at his workshop in Scotland and he was having to relocate. I bought a unit in Scotland to keep Bert's business going and that was the starting point for passenger rolling stock from Just Like the Real Thing to go with the locomotives.

One of the carriage designs I really wanted was GWR 'Toplights', but the body was too complicated which meant they couldn't be made in etch. I did all the research with John Lewis – an expert on GWR carriages – and got all the drawings and started drawing up the Third and the Brake Composite, but I also wanted the restaurant car and the full brake, but it wasn't happening fast enough.

At the time, Bert's design methods were focused on 2D, which had served him well. But as 3D CAD became essential, we needed to bring in new tools and skills to meet the demands of the 'Toplights' and BR Mk 1s for Leamington Spa. I couldn't get Bert to produce Mk 1s, and we were seven or eight months into running the business with just the Gresley teaks and the first of the 'Toplights' out but the Mk 1s were getting nowhere.

Through the advert I found a modeller in Dundee who worked in 3D CAD. He came down to the factory and spent some time with Bert and expressed concern that projects weren't suited to 2D CAD. Bert was such a clever engineer he had worked out how to do the tumblehome and roofs using clingfilm. He had moulds and would take the resin parts, wrap them tight with clingfilm over a former and that gave him the correct shape without the need to tool it.

But the Mk 1s had five arcs and were too complex for that method. We had to change, upgrade all the software to 3D using Solidworks and brought in a new designer

Making the masters for each mould was the most painstaking of tasks – and it could all go wrong in an instant if there was a spike in the power. Here a Class 37 cab is being carved out of Sika tooling board to make a master for a new kit. *Pete Waterman.*

GWR 'King' 6004 *King George III* is amongst Pete's favourite 'O' gauge models. This BR lined blue 4-6-0 was built from the upgraded Malcolm Mitchell 7mm scale kit with new backhead fittings, slide bars and underframe. *Mike Wild.*

who could operate 3D CAD in Lawrie Lynch. Lawrie had mould making experience in its biggest form having worked in the ship building industry.

Solidworks was incredibly expensive, but I gave Laurie the tools and said I want the best. "I want you to shake the box and it all falls together as a kit with superglue" was my instruction. That was the whole point of what I wanted from JLTRT – it had to be as simple to build as an Airfix kit. Whatever I gave Lawrie he would get it done and make it to the very highest standard.

When we came to the diesels, we needed far more detail than ever we had needed before because they were all different. Bogie differences, roof differences, cab differences all had to be catered for. For example, I couldn't just do one model for the 'Peaks' – there were six cabs, six roofs, six floors, and that could work out at £75k just for the patterns to make the moulds.

I remember setting a price of £450 per kit, but that was probably looking at it costing around £100 more per kit that was ever made above the sale price. It was the lost wax brass castings that really killed us – it was so expensive. For example, the 'WD' 2-8-0 was sold for £450 as a kit, but it was costing me £750 to produce the parts to go into the box! In the 'WD' alone there was 2kg of lost wax brass castings.

Steam locomotives are another big challenge when it comes to kits. Again the traditional way had been to use etched metal for the chassis, where the parts are straight, but the boilers were typically made from white metal which is where you got the

Looking over the Just Like the Real Thing workshop, the size of the machinery involved in creating these high detail kits is clear to see. *Pete Waterman.*

weight from. However, we wanted to be able to put a steam locomotive boiler together in one piece. It wasn't simple as there are different parts that must be considered – the straight smokebox, straight or parallel boiler then you've got either a round or Belpaire firebox shape to consider too.

However, the biggest problem we had when wanting to move to cast resin boilers was weight. You needed 3.5kg in a steam locomotive to make it run the way it should and haul scale length trains. The solution was to make a white metal core over which the resin is poured to make the boiler mould. Even so, while 3D design can do the basic shape all the rivets, washout plugs, feeds and covers had to be added to the mould by hand. In that boiler you are looking at the best part of

six weeks work to create a single pattern, but when you get it right every single one is the same and they all weigh 3.5kg.

COMPUTER CONTROL

CNC (Computer Numerical Control) machines were used by JLTRT. The first one was just for the cabs which was a five-axis CNC machine with a rotating head. Making the cab was technical for the diesels. We'd put a block of tooling board in, and the CNC carved out the cab including the inside shape and all the detail on the outside based on the 3D CAD design which Lawrie and his team created. It was a five-axis machine which meant we could get the cab spot on.

This was the process to make the masters which would then allow the mould to be

The 'Peak' diesels were the first step into the diesel market for JLTRT and revealed just how complex is would be to replicate these locomotives correctly. D31 poses on Hatton Bank in BR economy green. *Mike Wild.*

Each diesel locomotive kit was built from a series of separate main assemblies – two cabs, a central body section and roof. Added to this were bogies and underframe tanks while hundreds of additional lost wax castings were included to add the final details to each model. This is a test sample of the Class 40 with split headcode boxes. *Mike Wild.*

created. The mould would allow up to 40 cabs to be produced before it needed to be remoulded from the master. Then you learned that you cannot mix your patterns – No. 1 cab always must be the No. 1 cab and if there was any damage or mistake, you had to recut it. The No. 2 end cab couldn't be used as a replacement.

The manufacturing process was incredibly expensive. The modeller at JLTRT had to polish the masters and add any final detailing to the Sika tooling board which was what tool makers used instead of steel. Tooling board is very hard wearing, but very fine to work with.

Once the master was made it was placed into a casting box where silicon is poured in and allowed to go solid. When you take the box off you have a solid block of silicon. Next you have to get the pattern out of the silicon

block which you do with very sharp scalpels. You have to be very careful when you do that as you need a perfect connection between the two parts of the mould.

The mould is now ready for use, but it can only be used for around 40 cabs as the heating effect of the resin burns the mould meaning that you need to go back to the master to make a new mould.

The second big CNC machine was a bed CNC which was used to do the coach sides, roofs and floors and was over 8ft long. It had a massive tooling block which went in to create the patterns for the carriages. It had seven different cutters on the head which would interchange as programmed.

It would start with a bold cutter to rough out the shape giving a flat and a tumblehome.

After which it would change tools and repass over the tooling block with different heads to add the fine detail. It could only work on one side of the pattern at a time until it reached a pickup point when the tooling block is turned over. This can take three or four days to complete just one of these patterns, but if there is a spike in the electric then all the work could be lost, and you'd have to start over again. The tooling board could cost up to £3,000 and you could lose a week's work in an instant.

That was the big difference - you now had highly skilled tool makers giving the modeller absolutely excellent quality which is unparalleled. You are talking about £3,500 to create one single mould for a boiler, and even then, it could go wrong and you might have to do it again. Multiply that by the number of separate parts in a kit and you can see how the costs go up quickly.

We wanted to take the idea of 3D design even further with the ultimate experiment being 3D printed locomotives as this new technology started to find its way into modelling. I did a GWR 'Dukedog' 4-4-0 and an Aspinall '2F' 0-6-0, but no one saw what we were doing as inspirational or different.

We were going down the route of 3D printing for the tools from CAD which would simplify the market and had the potential to make 'O' gauge more accessible. We tried out different methods which could even have created single piece bodies with superb detail. A boiler would take seven days to print, but even so it would still have cost £5,000 for the tools because it needed a £150,000 machine to make that quality of print and even the resin for the 3D printing process cost £650 per kilogram.

A GWR '4575' 2-6-2T leads a pair of auto carriages down Hatton Bank – all three items have been built from kits from the JLTRT range to recreate this accurate formation. *Mike Wild.*

The first steam locomotive kit designed afresh by JLTRT was the Stanier rebuilt 'Royal Scot' 4-6-0. 46148 *The Manchester Regiment* was the first to be built and finished to launch the kit. *Mike Wild.*

THE JLTRT CATALOGUE

Over the years JLTRT produced a huge range of locomotives, rolling stock and accessories. Steam locomotives included GWR '45XX' and '4575' 2-6-2Ts, the ex-Malcolm Mitchell 'King' 4-6-0, '56XX' 0-6-2T, 'Panniers', the GWR '517' 0-4-2T, Collett 'Grange' 4-6-0 and Hawksworth 'Modified Hall', the GWR heavy freight 2-8-0Ts in original Churchward and later Collett forms amongst others.

Eric Underhill's kits continued in the range, upgraded with resin boilers, including those for the Midland '2F' 0-6-0 and Fowler '4F' 0-6-0 which were joined by the likes of the Stanier 'Black Five' 4-6-0, rebuilt 'Royal Scot' and even an Aspinall Class 23 0-6-0ST.

When it came to diesels, we had them all. From the Class 17s and 20s to the full set of Western Region hydraulics and Class 37s, 'Peaks' and 47s we made top quality kits which modellers could build. We even made the Blue Pullman power cars.

Some of the locomotives were chosen because they were specific to Leamington and my own memories. We did the North British D600 'Warships' because I saw them all at Leamington when they stopped for a crew change on their way down from NBL to Swindon. They were all hauled by a '5100' 2-6-2T from Crewe to Swindon where they were then inspected and accepted into traffic by the Western Region. We did all versions of the NBL 'Warship' and while it was available it was a popular kit.

The carriage range expanded to cover Gresley corridor carriages, GWR 'Toplights' stock plus the BR Mk 1 and Mk 2 carriages, but freight wagons was where we always saw great results.

But the market was changing again. Ready-to-run 'O' gauge was taking off and even though we had the best kits possible the JLTRT Class 47 – my favourite locomotive –

had competition from China at a price that we couldn't compete with. We had to call it a day with JLTRT, though the kits continued under MM1 models until 2022.

COMBINING METHODS

Freight stock is a passion for me. I'm always building new rolling stock. Because I'm fascinated by wagons, I had already gone down a route of doing a series of vans including all the BR, LNER and SR 10-12ton box vans. My aim was that you could literally have built any type of box van. The reason we could do that was they all used 3D printed moulds.

This meant we could make them quite cheaply compared with CNC tool making. That's where I saw the future and you could add as much detail as you wanted. Because I was a fanatic I wanted every detail, but not everyone wanted that, and they could choose.

Some wagons were outstanding like the Presflo and Prestwin cement wagons - we could never make enough of those - and they became a focus because they always sold, but some of the vans were less popular.

We came to a series of technical problems and the real problem with resin which was thickness. I started off my career with white metal and I knew how to get around that problem which was to shape it. During lockdown the last thing I did for JLTRT was a 21ton mineral and this is where technology hit the buffers. There was no way we could get enough out of a mould to make it work and to get what I wanted into production. Lawrie was getting 70% rejection because you

couldn't cast it because the body was too fine, they just kept warping. There was no problem on a box van, you can't see the thickness, its hidden inside, but not on an open wagon – everything is on show. To do the 21ton body was beyond the way we were casting.

I wanted 50 of these but only got 10 because of the failures. I could cast the chassis and then went back to my early days with Peco

Wonderful Wagons and laser-cut the bodies from timber and plasticard parts to go onto a cast chassis with white metal details. By going backwards, I started a whole new world of possibilities by combining the new technology of laser cutting and 3D printing with a cast chassis featuring white metal accessories.

This way forward works for the right type of vehicle, and I even went on to produce every

To demonstrate the detail of the GWR 'Toplight' carriage models at shows, JLTRT had samples built with cutaways to show the interior. The combination of resin body parts together with etched and lost wax brass parts coupled with white metal castings made them exceptional. *Mike Wild.*

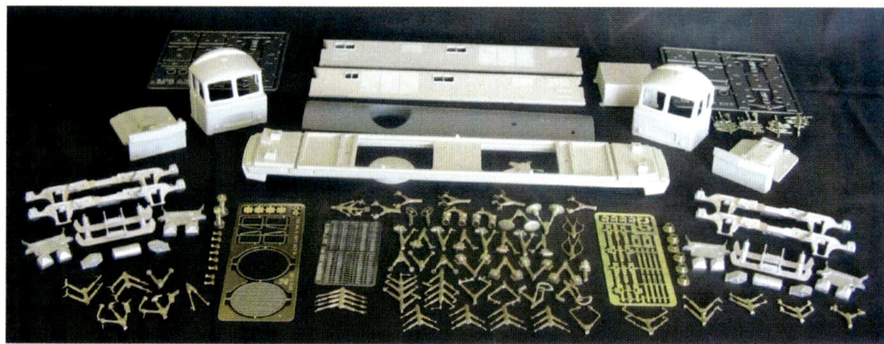

Illustrating the volume of parts in a JLTRT kit is this image of the 'Hymek' for 7mm scale. *JLTRT.*

Steam locomotives needed weight and JLTRT found a clever way to achieve this with resin boilers. A metal core was created for each boiler which ensured the kit could reach the 3.5kg target for a finished locomotive. *Mike Wild.*

This sample of the LMS pioneer diesel bodyshell illustrates how detailed the tools for the JLTRT models were. This kit was designed for ease of assembly, like all others, but had hundreds of hours invested in making the right tools for its parts. *Mike Wild.*

The NBL D600 'Warships' were another popular JLTRT kit. Pete saw all of these locomotives on delivery at Leamington Spa. The kit on the other hand catered for all variations on these A1A-A1A hydraulics. *Mike Wild.*

Lost wax parts were cast with trees allowing multiples to be cast in one go. *Pete Waterman.*

The Bert Collington Gresley teak carriages were a game changer for 'O' gauge modellers. Individual differences, correct body profiles and roofs and simple construction were the hallmarks. *Mike Wild.*

type of Siphon G from laser-cut parts during 2020 to see how far I could push laser-cutting in making scale rolling stock.

The big difference is price - the combination of modelling methods makes these so much more cost effective. Something that would have cost £140 in resin would now be little more than £20-£30 by combining the materials. This change in price for me brought 'O' gauge back

into contention – the scale isn't about buying what's made for you - it's about building what you want and with new technology we had the potential to make it affordable too.

Probably the most famous of the wagons I've built this way are the 'Sealions' and 'Seacows' which have laser-cut wood and plasticard bodies which can be cut in less than 20 minutes. You can build them in a couple of

hours then all you need are the cast bogies, wheels and final details to bring them to life. This is what 'O' gauge is all about: building models and creating unique trains.

I still believe there are people out there that want the Just Like The Real Thing kits. They were designed to be built and are still to this day a symbol of quality in 7mm scale modelling. ■

Freight stock is a passion for Pete, especially box vans with the huge range of variations. These are bodies for BR 12ton (front) Southern plywood 12ton (top left) and LNER 10ton planked (top right) vans. The advantage of a box van is the shape could hide any thickness of material required for strength. *Mike Wild.*

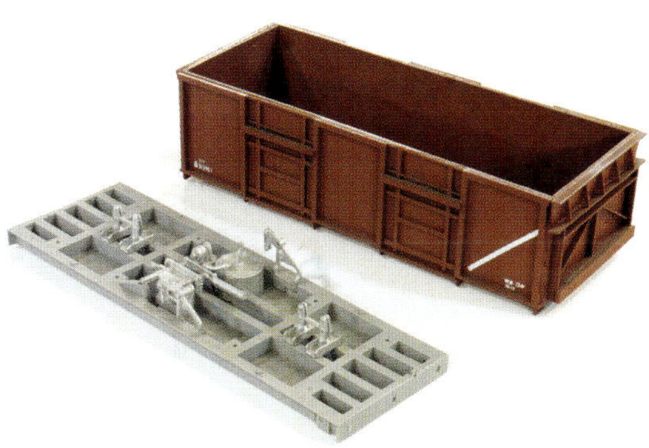

Building 21ton mineral wagons proved to be a challenge with traditional resin castings, as they needed to be too thin to suit this method. Switching to a laser-cut body with a cast resin chassis solved all the problems, similar to the early Peco Wonderful Wagon kits of the 1950s. *Mike Wild.*

'Seacow' and 'Sealion' wagons were another project for Pete which combined laser-cutting for the bodies with cast parts for the bogies, bufferbeam draw gear and other details showing the way forward for 'O' gauge kits. *Mike Wild.*

The power of 3D printing was explored by JLTRT towards the end of Pete's time with the business including complete locomotive bodies like this Aspinall '2F' 0-6-0. Could this have been the future and a way to bring new people into 'O' gauge? *Mike Wild.*

Sell Your Collection

TRUST OUR EXPERTS

CUSTOMER FRIENDLY, DOWN TO EARTH APPROACH

ABOUT US

For over a decade, Ellis Clark Trains has been purchasing model railways, die-cast vehicles and railwayana – including some of the largest single-owner collections the market has seen.

We travel widely to value collections but can also make offers based on lists sent to us via email or post. With specialist knowledge of 7mm finescale O gauge as well as Continental and American models, we purchase all scales from all eras.

You'll find us friendly, professional and down-to-earth, and we'll work with you to understand your needs. So give us a call or drop us an email to discuss the next step in finding a new home for your trains. And in case you're wondering... **Albert is the dog**.

Contact us today
We'd love to hear from you

info@ellisclarktrains.com | **01756 701451** | ellisclarktrains.com

FAMILY BUSINESS

FRIENDLY SERVICE

PRE-OWNED &
SECOND HAND

WANTED CASH OR EXCHANGE

BUY · SELL · EXCHANGE · ANY GAUGE · ANY AGE

LOCOS - COACHES - WAGONS - TRACK-WORK - CONTROLLERS - ACCESSORIES
DIE-CAST - LORRIES - BUSES - PLANES - SOLDIERS - RAILWAYANA - AND MORE

DECEASED ESTATES - EX SHOP STOCK A SPECIALITY
FAST SERVICE WITH COMPLETE DISCRETION ASSURED

WE VALUE YOUR COLLECTION VERY HIGHLY!

1 CONTACT US
get in touch by email, phone or post with your list of items

2 OUR OFFER
our friendly staff will review your list and make an honest valuation offer

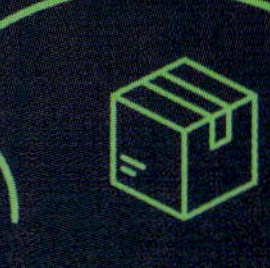

3 PACKAGE
either visit the shop, send us your items, or we can collect larger collections

4 PAYMENT!
fast, secure payment via your choice on confirming of the value offer – easy!

IMMEDIATE PAYMENT IN 4 EASY STEPS

GUARANTEED TOP PRICES PAID

Ref: WATERMAN25

DON'T DELAY - GET IN TOUCH TODAY!

📞 **+44 (0)114 255 1436**   ✉ **secondhand@railsofsheffield.com**

OR VISIT OUR WEBSITE AND CLICK ON THE 💷 Stuff to Sell? LINK:

www.railsofsheffield.com

PROUD WINNERS OF THESE RECENT AWARDS:

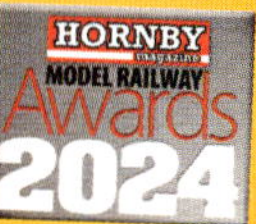

Layout of a lifetime

'O' gauge and Leamington Spa are what Pete Waterman is best known for in railway modelling. **PETE WATERMAN** introduces the layout and Mike Wild take a full tour of his amazing 'O' gauge model of Leamington Spa, Hatton Bank and Brinklow, illustrated here with unseen images. Photography, Mike Wild

It's more than 20 years since construction of Leamington Spa started. The story starts as I moved out of my building in London after 15 years and started to build a new one. At the same time I was starting a new business on the railway with the purchase of the first part of the BR Special Trains unit and was about to embark on a TV career with a documentary about ABBA for ITV which first aired in 1999. I never thought about it - just went and did it - and this turned my world upside down.

Pop Idol came next at the beginning of the 2000s and shortly after I was asked by a production company to talk to them about my love of railways. I had just started to write a book about BR and took what I had along. The meeting went well, and they said they would look at the book, or more what I'd written, and come back to me. The next day I had a phone call from them. They seemed surprised about my knowledge of BR. They said that Channel 4 wanted the show, so they were sending a guy over to work with me. They wanted three parts, five minutes long each. One part was to be about the birth of the railway - the Stockton and Darlington and the Liverpool to Manchester Railway. I'd never been that interested in this period at all - too early for my liking.

The part I really wanted to do, and why I had started the book, was from 1940 and the role the railways played in the Second World War and the start in 1947 of British Railways. They weren't interested in that period and at this point, I went cold on the whole thing and just got on with life.

A couple of weeks later, the producer got back in touch with a compromise: we would do four shows and it would be called *Trains with Pete Waterman*; and the question came back could I do the early years? So, I said yes, I could even though it wasn't by primary area of interest. It was great fun, and I loved every minute of it - the interviews, the footage they found, and the day filming on the railway.

At Leamington Spa shed GWR '74XX' 0-6-0PT 7427 is readied for departure with an engineering train while the yard is busy tending to steam and diesel traction.

Region:	Western/Midland
Period:	1950s-1960s
Gauge:	'O', 32mm
Scale:	7mm:1ft
Size:	85ft x 45ft
Control:	DCC, MERG

Fowler 'Patriot' 45506 powers up the gradient out of Leamington Avenue station with a long rake of Stanier 57ft corridor stock. This is the Midland side of Leamington with the Western Region station to the left.

"All it took was a mixed traffic black lined 'Hall' with red name and number plates, shining copper and brass to set me on a lifelong mission of modelling everything Great Western."

PETE WATERMAN OBE

The four parts were titled *Rocket Science*, *The Golden Age*, *How Trains Won the War* and *High Speed Revolution*. I enjoyed it; Channel 4 didn't. That's television.

I moved on. Then about two weeks later, ITV showed the ABBA documentary I had done. My phone went mad - they were over the moon, a record audience for a Wednesday, great - but I hadn't watched it! Then I got a call from Claude at ITV, who was the head and responsible for Pop Idol. "Had I done any other documentaries like this?" I told her about the Channel 4 series. She said she'd look at it but nothing about railways. She rang me back later and told me it was to be shown from Sunday and added, "We love it." I had done a lot of research into the programmes, and because I was invested in the real railway, I believe I had an insight that lots of historians did not, so it had come out from a new angle.

The thing that has always interested me was the people that made it work. So that was my focus. In the last episode, I finished on Leamington Spa station with "I'm off to build a model of Leamington." It was just a spur-of-the-moment comment, a throwaway line that popped into my head. The audience response shocked us all. It may have been a throwaway line, but I now wanted to make it happen.

GROUP PROJECT

Again, I was having a lot of work done on my house and had builders working on my barn - well, a carpenter actually. I had been recommended a carpenter from Manchester who had built baseboards for his layout - his name was Dave Douglas - and the story of Leamington began. We looked at 10mm Gauge One, but even with the size of my barn, little could be achieved, so 'O' gauge was the logical choice to meet the space available and the level of detail that I wanted to achieve.

Dave came up with the idea of asking at the Manchester club if anyone was interested in joining me in building a layout in my barn. We soon had seven of us. It was the size that was the thing as realism meant scale length trains, platforms, scenery, buildings, the works. All of the group were experienced modellers, the challenge was the thing, as what I wanted to do was very new to 'O' gauge: to run a summer Saturday service between 1947 and 1960. I approached Dick Blenkinsop, who was a local photographer, as I had all his books that heavily featured Leamington as he had a lineside pass. Dick was as enthusiastic as us which helped keep the ball rolling for this mighty project.

A Fowler 'Patriot' 4-6-0 works up the gradient from Avenue station with an express to pass a Stanier 'Mogul' with a ballas train. In the distance Leamington Spa shed can be seen.

The garage and town houses dominate the foreground as BR '9F' 2-10-0 92001 disturbs the peace at the head of a fish train on the Midland.

All of the signals are fully operational and built to replicate the real location in exacting detail. GWR 'Hall' 4904 Binnegar Hall is ready to depart with an inter-regional working formed of Maunsell stock.

Dave was already well into the barn work and had replaced the doors, so we had a warm, big barn to work in, but first things first - we fitted a kitchen to make the tea! Now, although I knew it was to be Leamington, a couple of the lads were not interested in Great Western, so we had to have a place where they could run and not see any GWR locomotives. So we split the layout on one side of the barn in two, with a partition down the centre. One side we had Hatton Bank GWR, and the other Brinklow LMS on the West Coast. By pure luck, the track work actually worked and, what's more, the guys got a scale LMS layout!

We then started to get Dave off on building the boards. Without a doubt, this is where Dave came into his own, his knowledge was key and made the rest of our work that much simpler.

The first thing once the boards were complete was to print out the track plan and paste it to the boards so we could lay the track on top. First, we put in the four main tracks all the way round. We had decided to use C&L track for the main lines and hand-build the points and crossovers, and Peco track and points in the storage yard. This meant we had four main lines to work with so that we could start to build the stock and test it out. We had all decided to go DCC as it was the only way we could run the layout properly, but DCC was in its infancy. Luckily for us, there was a guy in the Manchester club way ahead of the field and was only too keen to get involved.

We already had some fantastic locomotives to test out the track, and I mean they were fantastic - but, and as it turned out, it was a big but - this layout was bigger than anyone at the time had built. Brilliant as they looked, running them on such a big layout gave us a problem. They all had big motors, but were all worm-on-wheel drive, and after a couple of circuits gave up the ghost. The only one that worked had a gearbox fitted. When we added stock, the weight of the engine proved to be too bit to light. The 'O' gauge standards recommended 3.5kg.

> *"My aim was to create a slice of railway through a town in the 1950s to show younger visitors what it was like back then, not just railway wise but the wider scene."*

PETE WATERMAN OBE

I had stated that the project could take up to twenty years to complete, and if we couldn't run every week, we'd lose interest - I'd seen this happen at most clubs. The answer was to close a circuit at a time and add the points and crossovers so we could run on the other; we ran these on DC. When that circuit was complete, we moved onto the other and did the same. We then went back to the first, closed that, and added the DCC, then closed that and added DCC to the last main line. It was at this point that we made a decision to be able to switch one line off so we could still run DC so visiting locomotives could take a turn on the layout without the need for a chip to be installed.

LEAMINGTON TODAY

Entering the room via the central staircase you are greeted by a view of Leamington Spa's distinctive houses and as you turn it takes a moment to let everything before you sink in. It's a stunning scene which spans more than 85ft from one end to the other and a maximum width of 45ft. There are off-scene storage sidings in two groups at one end which allow a full set of trains to be prepared for running days, while around one side and even underneath there are more storage tracks hidden from view.

But what was the appeal of the location for Pete? "I was born in Coventry and grew up there. I was bitten by the GWR bug very early on. I was taken by my mum and Auntie Ginnie

On Hatton Bank BR '9F' 2-10-0 92150 has paused in the loop to allow a passenger working to pass while a pair of GWR 'Castle' 4-6-0s thunder towards Leamington with an express.

to see my Uncle Ernie who used to go fishing every Tuesday on the River Leam and they would let me sit at the station trainspotting until they picked me up later - you could do this back then. My mum would have been locked up if it was today. All it took was a mixed traffic black lined 'Hall' with red name and number plates, shining copper and brass to set me on a lifelong mission of modelling everything Great Western."

The aim of the project was to create something new in 7mm scale. Pete's group of modellers were all experienced, but at that time there were few really large 'O' gauge layouts, particularly on the scale that was imagined for this layout. "The space that we had was quite unique," adds Pete. "The planning was left for me to do."

The location had a number of appeals in that it had separate stations for the ex-GWR

and ex-LNWR lines named General and Avenue respectively (there was a third, but that was deemed too confusing to include) while it also boasted a raised position through the town which meant the line went in front and behind buildings which acted to block the view of the trains. The inclusion of the GWR and LNWR lines also meant there could be two separate double track main line around the full circuit to cater for different tastes in the group.

GAUGING CHOICE

The choice of scale wasn't as straightforward as you might think. There was no rolling stock at the start of the project which offered a blank slate. "I had a large selection of 10mm (Gauge 1) models, which we did look at, but it really didn't work and I wanted more detail than in 4mm:1ft scale. Two of the guys had some 7mm stuff so after a few beers, 'O' gauge it was."

Construction of Leamington Spa, Hatton Bank and Brinklow was a big task from the outset which required a lot of planning. "This is where technology kicked in," enthuses Pete. "I had lots of high-tech stuff at the time in my studios and my railway business. This meant we could do all the track work in CAD and then make it fit the boards, or was it the other way round?"

"The one thing on my mind was scale - not the feet and inches type, but the overall scale.

At Brinklow Stanier '8F' 2-8-0 48016 takes a mineral train towards Leamington Spa as it passes the goods shed. This area of the layout is still a work in progress with future plans to develop it further.

What did it feel like, did it balance? Having spent over half of my working life in film and television studios I knew that if it looked right then it is right. You must trick the eye into seeing one thing but making it believe it's something else - it's called false perspective."

Original plans helped greatly in development of the layout. At the outset Pete was given two sets of plans – a full rating plan for the railway from 1954 which covered the whole layout about to be modelled, and a full set of drawings for General and Avenue stations. "The Avenue plans were fantastic and still on cloth and hand shaded," Pete added.

"I decided from day one that the station buildings had to be scale so as to achieve my false perspective. I had a very large laser cutting machine, which made it very easy to make these fantastic buildings, once the design was done. Pete continues: "The first problem was that the team that did this were not modellers, so there was no false perspective! It's all very well having every rafter and every tile in the right place, but if it doesn't look right then what is the point? This all meant we had to remake a lot of the station as we built it, which sort of defeated the point of using CAD. However, we decided to teach ourselves to use CAD which changed everything."

Another early decision was adoption of Digital Command Control (DCC) to operate the layout, but Pete adds: "The fact was that DCC did not do what it was claimed to do." He explains: "What do I mean by that? There is no feedback on DCC. If you change a point and it shows you it's changed, it does not actually mean it has, and that is a problem - a safety critical one – especially on a model railway the size of Leamington Spa which covers nearly 90ft x 50ft with areas of the railway completely out of sight to operators in certain positions."

"The real railway cannot operate with safety critical problems. It needs confirmation that an action has been completed successfully - that the point has changed and is locked in the new position. It sounds easy now 20 years later, but it wasn't back then." Then there was the problem of accommodating analogue locomotives. "There were still more analogue than DCC locomotives which visited the layout," Pete adds "so we had to have a way of switching one circuit to analogue while the rest still used DCC. Oh how things have changed - it's very rare now that we use that facility."

Working as a team has been essential to build Leamington Spa, as Pete explains: "Let me just say that the key factor I had which was critical in all we did or were trying to do, were the members of the Manchester Model Railway Club who were all part of our original team - and what a team they were! They had been there, done that, got the t-shirt and moved on.

THROUGH THE TOWN

In building the layout Pete's aim was to create a slice of railway through a town in the 1950s.

2020 saw replacement of the original goods shed model with this much more imposing new structure. The baseboard was expanded to make way for the building.

BR '9F' 2-10-0 92150 pauses in the loop on Hatton bank with its long goods. Each wagon has been modelled correctly with unique features to bring interest to this mixed working.

Leamington Spa's stunning Art Deco station building, originally built by the GWR in 1937-1939, has been modelled to scale in 7mm scale for the layout.

"I tell people I'm a railway modeller and that's my thing, it's the doing for me that's the magic."

PETE WATERMAN OBE

"I wanted to show younger visitors what it was like back then, not just railway wise but the wider scene." Pete continues: "At first the priority was to get the railway running properly which meant we could be sure that when we switched it on everything worked, stayed on the track, and we could take for granted that it would run. So far so good."

A layout as large as Leamington Spa absorbs a lot of track and materials. The main lines contain more than 1,000ft of track in the running lines and there is around the same amount of track again in the crossovers and sidings. "How do you keep 2,000ft of track clean?" questions Pete. "It may sound like heresy, but you don't. You can't. It's actually worse because you have locomotive, wagon and carriage wheels in the thousands to keep clean. My advice? Forget it: you are never going to keep up with the task and still enjoy what you've built. So from day one we had an only clean when you need attitude to the problem. If it's working, let it."

"Lockdown in March 2020 was perfect timing for us as it meant that we could work safe from home! We could work seven days a week in isolation. This meant I could really get stuck into the main task that was left - the town centre." This was prime modelling time for Pete who loves to get stuck into his projects whether they are buildings, locomotives or rolling stock. He continues: "I had the rating plans and I had over the years taken hundreds of photographs all around the station and town so I had a good idea what the task was. I then started to use the website Britain From Above. This site has aerial photographs taken of the whole of Britain from about 1920 to the early 1950s. With this site and all my photographs I was able to start to build the town."

"At first I started with the shells to see how they fitted into the space I had, always asking whether it looked right. A lot of the time I was having to work out the scale of the buildings for the false perspective. This, I have to say, is a lot harder than it sounds and sometimes meant I built some structures two or three times, much to the annoyance of the CAD team." That's dedication to the cause! "All this is best shown in the goods shed. Like all of us, I had bought a shed that sort of fitted the bill and had been in place for years. Nobody had said anything that bad or even pointed out it was from the wrong railway company, but this is where false perspective comes in to its own. Let me explain."

"If you stand back from something and look at it as an overall picture you see it balances out. Even small gaps become important, so if small gaps are important then large buildings by the same rule must become very

Attention to detail extends to every part of this layout be it rolling stock, trackwork, buildings or figures. In the sidings at Leamington stands a Flatrol wagon loaded with a Ruston Bucyrus excavator.

A rare view from the rear of Leamington as a Stanier 'Mogul' leads an engineering train along the Midland while a 'Pannier' takes charge of a second permanent way train on the Western route. All around the railway the town sets the scene.

important. Standing back from the layout one morning and looking at the model as a whole, not as a collection of buildings, the scale and weight of the goods shed shouted at me how wrong it looked in the overall view. Yes it was false perspective, but it was the wrong false perspective. It just didn't balance in the wider view. So what to do? Cheat. We added a new front extension to the layout and built the proper shed in its place. We had the drawings and loads of great photographs, but it still didn't look spot on, so by using 3D CAD we were able to work it out.

"The lesson in simple terms is that you're unlikely to get a fabulous looking station like Leamington with a small goods shed. Why would the real railway do that? If the station was important enough to be rebuilt at what must have been a large cost why would a small goods shed makes any sense? The real railway never wasted money on anything."

SCALE TRAINS

Just as important as the scenery, and perhaps more so in some respects, were the trains that would run on the layout. "From day one it's always been our intention to run scale trains at scale speeds, which isn't to everybody's taste, but that's what we wanted." For Pete it was about those captivating moments as

a young spotter and being able to recreate them in miniature. "To see an '8F' 2-8-0 or a 'Super D' 0-8-0 on a 60-wagon coal train was what we were trying to capture, to take us back in time to when we stood and watched this for real - the noise, the smell: all you needed for this were your own memories and imagination. There's also a fun side here and the challenge is to locomotive builders - to take our 60-wagon loaded coal train round the LMS track as slow as you can. Our record is 1 hour 12 minutes. DCC chips are allowed, but no stay alives or flywheels to assist."

Criteria were set for locomotives and rolling stock early on in the projects development

'WD' 2-8-0 90585 thumps through the centre road at Leamington Spa with a long rake of BR 21ton mineral wagons.

to ensure everything was built to a similar standard. "Locomotives should be around 3kg in weight and have motors with gearboxes as well as split pick-ups with ZIMO decoders. Coaches should have shackle or buckeye couplings with Slater's wheels. Wagons must have realistic and accurate three-link or Instanter couplings with Slater's or Peartree wheels."

The rolling stock roster has been assembled over many years and now includes all classes which would have run through Leamington Spa in the period of the model and the correct identities too. Amongst the fleet you will find ex-GWR 'Hall', 'Castle', 'King', and 'Grange' 4-6-0s, 'Small Prairie' 2-6-2Ts, 'Panniers', '42XX' 2-8-0Ts, '72XX' 2-8-2Ts, Western Region hydraulics and DMUs on the Western. The Midland fleet includes 'Patriot' and 'Royal Scot' 4-6-0s, Stanier '8F' 2-8-0s, ex-LNWR 'Super D' 0-8-0s, Stanier 'Moguls', BR '9F' 2-10-0s, 'WD' 2-8-0s and an array of diesel locomotives too.

The rolling stock is almost entirely kit built to replicate the amazing collection of carriages and wagons which would once have run through Leamington Spa. That includes scale length passenger workings – the Midland set of Mk 1s headed by LMS twins 10000 and 10001 is always popular – while the goods stock includes scale length coal trains, van trains, mixed goods, ballast workings, engineering trains and more. All of these are arranged in two separate storage yards at one end of the railway room, but naturally there is more stock than there is space for on the rails. To accommodate this an additional storage system with large cassettes has been developed to allow additional trains to be stored and loaded onto the layout when required.

TEAM EFFORT

"Now, you might gain the impression that I did all of this myself - but that couldn't be further from the truth," says Pete. "I am only part of the team. A leader I may be, but more importantly, I'm a member of a fantastic team of modellers. Not all are with us today as we get close to the end of what has been an amazing 20 years, so it seems appropriate to pay full credit to the 'Boys of Leamington Spa.'"

"In no particular order they are Dave Douglas, Mike Rathby, Les Fram, Geoff Holland, Roger Healey, Steve Corkery, Geoff Holt, Dave Baker, Arthur Magee, Dave Burns, Chris Louth, Roger Markland, Dave Jenning, Pete Thompson, Ron Chaplin, Andy Littler, Mike Taylor, Andy Gyde, Michelle Davidson,

Steve Fay, Paul Hanna, Paul Waterman, Peter Waterman jnr, Bob Tatman, Harrold Stephenson, John Dutton and Dave Geen.

"We have many friends who have helped along the way. There are so many funny days and also some sad days, but I guess that's how life works. I still have a bit to do to finish the job. I'm not one that says it's never done, but it will be finished before I go. We may add more detail but only we should know what that detail is.

"Things have changed so much in the last 20 years, some for the better and some not – it all depends on what you want from modelling, and all our needs are different. I tell people I'm a railway modeller and that's my thing, it's the doing for me that's the magic." ∎

A North British Type 2 hydraulic eases a set of fuel wagons out of the sidings at Leamington shed in the company of an all black English Electric 350hp shunter.

LEAMINGTON SPA TRACKPLAN *NOT TO SCALE*

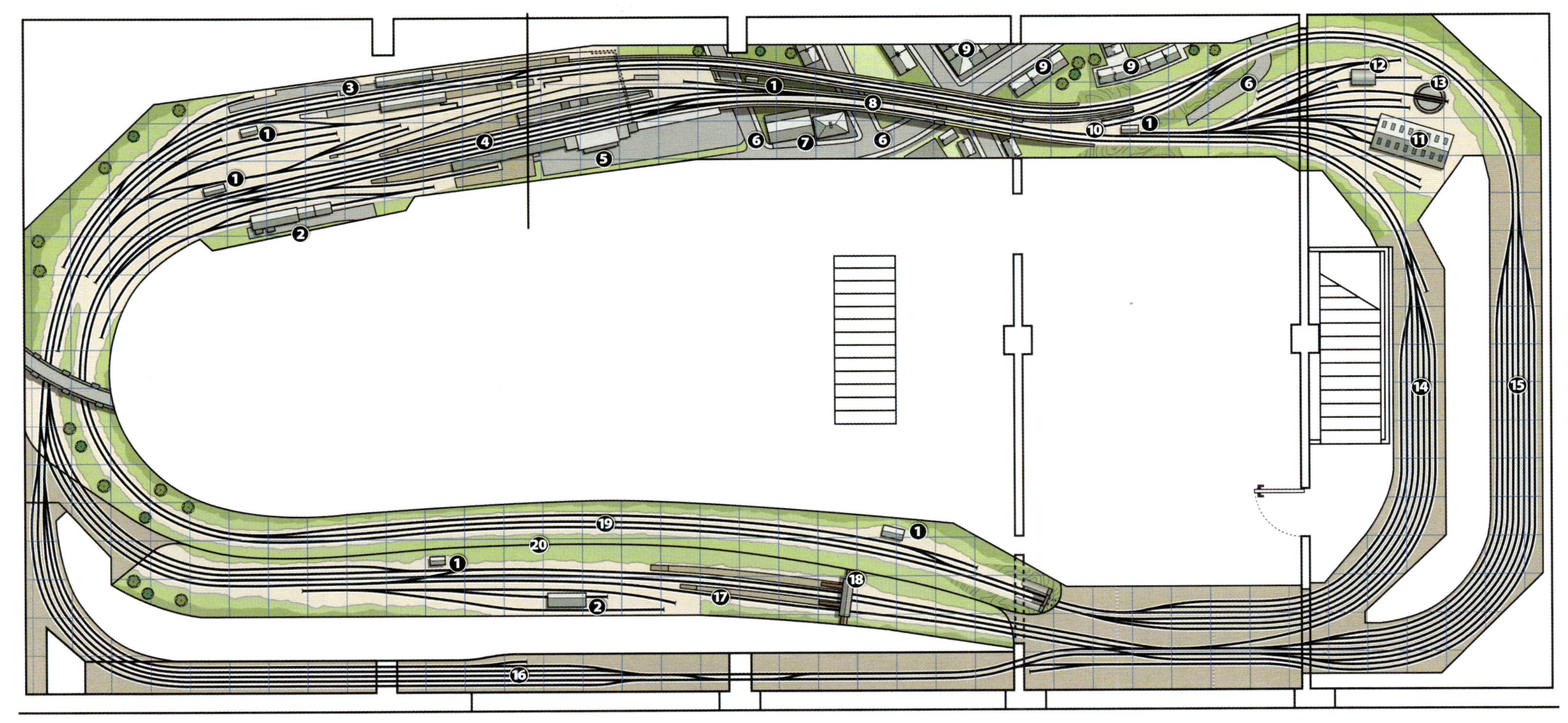

KEY

1. Signalbox	7. Car dealership	14. WR storage yard
2. Goods shed	8. Viaduct	15. LMR storage yard
3. Leamington Spa Avenue (LMR)	9. Houses	16. Off-scene train storage
4. Leamington Spa General (WR)	10. Line link	17. Brinklow
5. Art deco station building	11. Engine shed	18. Station building
6. Road	12. Coal stage	19. Hatton Bank
	13. Turntable	20. Back scene

A pair of freights headed by a 'Super D' 0-8-0, modelling the National Collection's 49395, and BR '9F' 2-10-0 92001 thread their way through the town on the approach to Leamington Spa station. This incredible scene has been 20 years in the making. *Mike Wild.*

Building Leamington

We delve into **PETE WATERMAN'S** archive of images to illustrate the early construction of Leamington Spa, Hatton Bank and Brinklow.

The baseboards were built by Dave Douglas. This is the view of the framework looking through Hatton Bank while Brinklow will take the left hand side of this area. *Pete Waterman.*

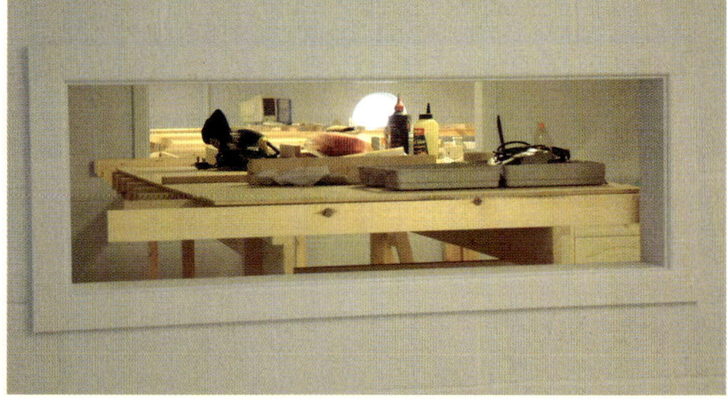

Construction of the layout included cutting holes through the new internal brick walls in the barn which houses Leamington Spa. These were finished and painted before layout construction started. *Pete Waterman.*

A central spine backscene was built between Hatton Bank and Brinklow to divide the GWR and LMS scenes. This is the view through Brinklow station. *Pete Waterman.*

The plain lines through Leamington General (left) and Avenue (right) are in place. To ensure the group could keep running trains, one line was taken out of use at a time to allow the pointwork to be installed. *Pete Waterman.*

In the storage yard Peco Streamline code 124 rail and points were used for speed and ease of construction. The formation has been laid out over a paper template to check it all fits as planned prior to the track being pinned down onto the baseboards. In the distance the main line through Hatton Bank is also being checked. *Pete Waterman.*

Pete lays the curves from Hatton Bank towards Leamington Spa on the GWR route using C&L Finescale track. The paper template behind shows the location of the Midland route to Brinklow. Templates were essential to ensure all the details of this huge 85ft long layout came together correctly. *Pete Waterman.*

Pointwork takes shape at the east end of Leamington Spa station. This complex arrangement mimics the real station in detail. *Pete Waterman.*

Leamington Spa station started out with four plain lines straight through using C&L track. These were later altered to include the correct track formation. *Pete Waterman.*

Leamington Spa South Signalbox is one of seven 'boxes on the layout. It was built specially for Leamington Spa the layout. *Pete Waterman.*

The backscene to Hatton Bank has been clad with MDF and a curved frame added at the scenic break. Beyond is the storage yard. *Pete Waterman.*

Scenery is coming together here as the stone tunnel portal and rock lines are modelled carefully to reflect the real location. *Pete Waterman.*

The link between the Western (nearest tracks) and Midland has been completed with the Midland climbing up a gradient into the main scenic section here. *Pete Waterman.*

The distinctive rail over road bridges were a complex task to complete for Leamington Spa, but one which was essential to its realism. *Pete Waterman.*

As well as building the layout Pete Waterman and his modelling friends made sure they enjoyed running trains on the developing layout including a challenge to see who could build the slowest running, most powerful locomotive. *Pete Waterman.*

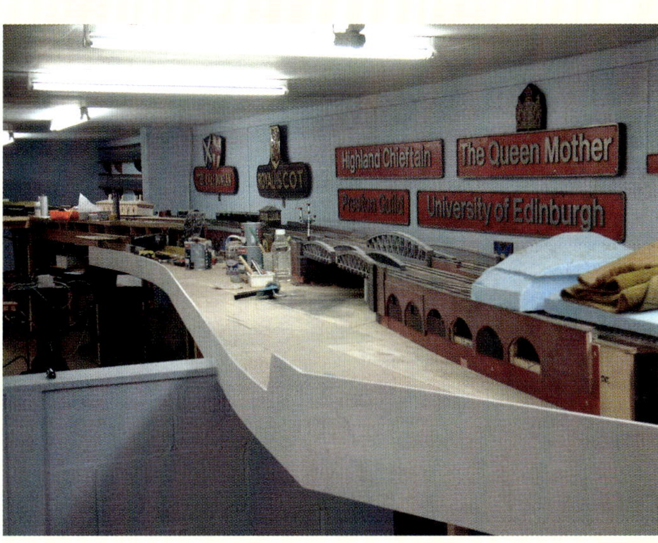

Scenery is coming together around the railway, but there are still many buildings to be created in this late 2000s image. *Pete Waterman.*

Avenue station building was scratchbuilt and finished with cast resin stone details and white metal canopy supports. *Pete Waterman.*

Hatton Bank's scenery is looking the part with ground cover, bushes and ballast all in place. Trees were starting to be added with more to come. The signals and signalbox were made specifically for the layout with the signals being fully operational so that the layout can be run like a proper railway. *Pete Waterman.*

Leamington Spa locomotive shed is installed by Dave Douglas. This image illustrates just how big this layout is with two people on top of the baseboards. *Pete Waterman.*

Construction of the town houses and structures started with clear plastic shells over which brick embossed plasticard was laid to create the final models. *Pete Waterman.*

CAVALEX
Models

For modellers, by modellers.

THE CLASS 60, BY CAVALEX

@cavalexmodels

www.cavalexmodels.com

Scan me for more information 

Bring **live** train information to your home with a UK Departure Board! Available in 3 sizes to display real time information for your local station or indeed any station - train, tram, bus or tube in the UK.

Each board is designed and built in Britain with the ability to perform real station announcements.

We use a variety of data sources to accurately show what is scheduled at a station in real time. Whether you are an enthusiast wanting to see the latest action or a commuter wanting to know if your train is arriving or delayed. A UK Departure Board can bring it to you!

Use **MAKINGTRACKS** for **5%** discount

DESKTOP DEPARTURES® BOARD

Measuring just **10.5cm x 4cm x 2cm** Have it on your desk or in the office. Available in a black or white case with a choice of 4 display colours!

Scan QR for more details

CLASSIC DEPARTURE BOARD

Measuring **60cm x 11.5cm x 3.5cm** Great for wall displays in your hall, study or hobby room. *As seen on the MakingTracks3 layout*

Scan QR for more details

PRO DEPARTURE BOARD

Measuring **100cm x 18cm x 4.5cm** Just like a real station board! Hang it on your wall for that great experience!

Scan QR for more details

Our customers love us!  Trustpilot

Making Tracks 1 was a bold step when Pete Waterman and the Railnuts took their new 64ft long 'OO' gauge layout to Chester Cathedral for the summer. With the superb stained-glass windows of the cathedral behind, a Class 66 leads a cement train out of Northchurch Tunnel as a Class 390 Pendolino enters. *Mike Wild.*

The second Making Tracks layout in 2022 took things to another level, literally. It modelled the grade separated Hillmorton Junction with a realistic 20ft long gradient. A Class 87 speeds along the lower level fast lines as a pair of Class 37s climb the gradient with cement wagons. *Mike Wild.*

One, two, three

Making Tracks burst onto the scene in 2021 with brand-new energy for the model railway scene. **PETE WATERMAN** explains the how the first three layouts came to be.

I t's funny how things work out. I had sold my Locomotive Works at Crewe and moved my full-size engines to Peak Rail and I was now working with the Government on Apprenticeships while chairing The Cheshire and Warrington LEP. Alongside all this I was Chair of the local transport board working on High Speed 2 at Crewe and was appointed to the board of directors for Transport for the North. Then seemingly out of nowhere, Covid hit.

Just before this I had been asked to meet the Dean of Chester Cathedral to give him some advice on an exhibition he was planning for the Cathedral to celebrate 150 years since the death of Thomas Brassey who was one of the great unsung heroes of the Industrial Revolution.

He was born in 1805 in Chester and was responsible for building over 6,500 miles of railway in the UK, Europe, India, Australia and Canada. He died in 1870 but was largely unknown and in the shadows of the likes of George Stephenson and Richard Trevithick. However, at Chester Cathedral there is a memorial to Thomas Brassey which was installed in 1879 to mark the Cheshire-born man's achievements.

Pete Waterman stands with Cefn Viaduct on the installation of Making Tracks 1 at Chester Cathedral in July 2021. *Richard Watson.*

The Cathedral had run a very successful LEGO display in 2019 and needed an annual attraction to bring visitors into the building to keep it going. Can you believe it costs £6,000 a day to keep Chester Cathedral open?

I was going in to give advice as the Dean had found a company to build a model railway for display at the Cathedral, but at a cost! I had a word with the Railnuts and offered to do the project for him. We started and then we all got locked down, but we had already built part of it.

In that time when we couldn't work on the layout for the Cathedral, I gave a lot of thought to it and was not happy at all so I rang the Dean and told him of my idea. "Why don't we build a massive model railway based on the West Coast as that would be fantastic."

He was taken back by the scale but thought it would work. We had decided to build it in 'OO' gauge, so I talked to Simon Kohler at Hornby who was as keen as me, so off we went.

It had to be a modern layout as I wanted to show the public that we could do something that they could see and travel on. I had no idea how big of a project it was and what the public would think. Part of the aim had been to show landmarks from the railway that were built by Thomas Brassey for a

"Why don't we build a massive railway based on the West Coast Main Line - that would be fantastic."

PETE WATERMAN OBE

connection to his memorial in the Cathedral. That included the Shugborough Tunnel and Cefn Viaduct which really stood out for their stone construction while other features included overhead electrification, Tring Cutting, North Church Tunnel and the north end of Watford Tunnel.

TRADITIONS

We set up Making Tracks 1 the way that every model show did with steel barriers in front to keep people behind them and on the second day the Dean and I agreed it wasn't right and that we should remove them and more importantly let people drive the trains themselves.

In the first year visitors had to drive from the inside of the layout as we had made use of an early ZIMO DCC control system that had wired controllers connected to the main base station. It was a challenging summer to keep those handsets working – I'm sure we spent more time fixing handsets than controlling trains with them – but nevertheless it was a huge success.

We'd done something completely different. We'd put model railways in the spotlight and hosted a public event in the summer of 2021 when the world was only just coming back out of lockdown. We borrowed rolling stock, made new friends and learnt a lot. We even had a dedicated BR blue running day on the last Friday of the first summer with stock from Mike Wild and Mark Chivers at *Hornby Magazine*.

Making Tracks 1 had set the tone. The Cathedral loved having the railway there and it was brilliant at bringing people of all ages and backgrounds into the Cathedral. That was one of the fascinating things and being a city centre location, we could also pull families in to see the Cathedral and get involved with modelling.

After Chester, Making Tracks 1 made one final appearance at the 2021 Great Electric Train Show – the first big post-Covid model railway exhibition – which started a connection with Key Publishing's modelling events.

MAKING TRACKS 2

The first layout was such a success that we were immediately looking at plans for a second layout. The Dean wanted us back in 2022 – there was no question there – and Phil Moreton had joined the Railnuts and came into his own with his knowledge of electronics, laser-cutting and 3D printing.

During the first summer we realised that people wanted to get involved, to drive the trains, and that became one of our focuses for Making Tracks 2 – to make it user friendly so that anyone could turn up and drive the trains.

With its four track main line Making Tracks 1 was an all action layout where electric and diesel traction ran side by side. A pair of Class 86s head south with a container train as a Class 390 Pendolino and the New Measurement Train head north. *Mike Wild.*

Making Tracks 2 under construction. The workshop space only allows a limited section to be assembled at a time. In the foreground is Hillmorton Junction while in the background is the opposite end of the scene. *Mike Wild.*

Pete Waterman has been hands on in every Making Tracks project and takes great pride in working with the group. Here he modifies ground cover on Making Tracks 2 in early 2022. *Mike Wild.*

But how could we do that? How would they understand a DCC handset, all those function buttons and how to select locomotives and drive a train?

Phil had already been creating designs for large electronic track circuit boards which would display the positions of the trains to the public on each side of the layout. This block detection was only the start though – the big thing was tablet control. Boy was that a hit! Sometimes we had a line of 20 or 30 waiting to drive, I think we had over one hundred people a day taking the controls and driving trains on Making Tracks 2 that summer.

The tablet control system was a stroke of genius for Making Tracks. We used the Roco Z21 base station to operate the trains which meant we could have a pair of tablets to drive trains on each circuit and the roster on each could be managed too so that only the trains on that circuit could be driven on its tablet.

This took away all the dangers, if you can call them that, of handing over the controls and for another thing all trains could be stopped with any tablet at the push of a button.

Making Tracks 2 was a bigger challenge compared to the first layout, and not just because we built it in six months. We pushed the boundaries by selecting on my spotting location on the West Coast Main Line (WCML) at Clifton Road Junction just outside Rugby. Here we followed what it looked like in the 1950s by modelling the Great Central Railway Birdcage bridges over the WCML together with the grade separated Hillmorton Junction on the approach to Rugby.

This took Making Tracks to a new level, literally. The gradient for the junction was over 20ft long and followed exactly how the real railway looked. We used driver's eye view videos to gather the lineside details where we couldn't see them from the lineside and started creating unique buildings. Phil was a huge asset here as he allowed a new level of detail to be incorporated into Making Tracks 2 with his skill in creating laser-cut buildings and structures, something that we would come to value even more in the next project.

Making Tracks 2 was another fantastic success. We had scale length trains representing the latest in WCML rolling stock and, as a throwback to my youth, a pair of 'Super Ds' on a long rake of four-wheel mineral wagons joined the roster too. We were wowed by the response, again, to the Avanti West Coast Pendolinos on the fast lines and continued by taking Making Tracks 2 to the 2022 Great Electric Train Show in October that year.

DEBRIEF

We were then back at the workshop debriefing after the second summer at Chester Cathedral when Mike Wild threw a spanner in the works. "It's good he said," referring to what we had built so far, "but people want a station, that's their connection with the railway and how the public always interacts with it first."

Well, if we were going to build a station – and up until this point I didn't want to – it had to be amazing and the only one I thought would work was Milton Keynes Central.

Phil was on it straight away and off we went and soon discovered how much more complicated it was going to be than what we had done before. It had to be bigger, wider and feature realistic buildings to make it work. We'd prided ourselves on modelling to scale with Making Tracks 1 and 2, as the 64ft length allowed us to model a scale mile, but scale was about to mean something altogether different with the third layout.

We used Google Maps and made field trips to Milton Keynes to understand how everything fitted together, and the reaction was even bigger than we had expected – Mike was right!

The buildings we created for Making Tracks 3 were out of this world. Phil designed giant structures for the station buildings, office block and car parks which the Railnuts then assembled. We hit on a fantastic finish to

The Pride Pendolino, a Hornby model, departs Milton Keynes Central as GBRf's Class 66 66779 *Evening Star* takes a car train through the slow lines. *Mike Wild.*

In July 2021 Making Tracks 1 started the journey to a world record – but at that time no one knew that was even possible. *Richard Watson.*

The Grand Challenge – October 2023, Milton Keynes. Its late in the evening on Friday October 13 and the Railnuts are still at work testing the layout to get it ready for the opening of the Great Electric Train Show. The team stood down at 2am having got everything working. *Mike Wild.*

make the mirror glass walls of the main office block above the station entrance and even had every single one of the tiny holes laser-cut into the south car park walls which gave us another distinctive structure.

There was the overhead. Aron had already gone the extra mile on Making Tracks 2 when he built a fully working overlap in 4mm scale which worked and had proper tensioners, but for Making Tracks 3 he excelled. He built unique masts, cut parts by hand from brass, built working tensioning assemblies and hundreds of registration arms to make it the most complex catenary system I think we'll ever see on a portable model railway.

Making Tracks 3 was a roaring success at Chester Cathedral, and we'd now become established as the big attraction each summer drawing in excess of 50,000 visitors through the doors during our time there. It was incredible and the response to Making Tracks

Technology has moved Making Tracks forward and made it possible to build the stunning layouts in short order. Pete Waterman looks on as Robin Fox, Peter Lund and Phil Moreton assemble the platforms for Milton Keynes Central from custom laser-cut parts. *Mike Wild.*

Every layout starts out with the track being laid, but for Making Tracks 3 structures like the platforms had to be created to ensure everything went together as planned. *Mike Wild.*

Baseboard expert Dave Douglas checks the alignment of two of the boards for Making Tracks 3 with Pete Waterman.

Pete marks up the scale plans for Making Tracks 3 on the floor between Leamington Spa and Hatton Bank. *Phil Moreton.*

The idea for Making Tracks The Grand Challenge started at the 2022 Great Electric Train Show with a question: how long could it be? *Mike Wild.*

Scale length trains representing the modern railway was the plan for Making Tracks. Pete wanted to make the railway recognisable to all those who visited it at the Cathedral. *Mike Wild.*

3 was unreal. We couldn't believe how much the visitors loved seeing it and again we had visitors driving the trains to take their turn controlling Pendolinos, Voyagers, HSTs and more. We also pushed the boundaries further with the rolling stock with custom finished models of the Avanti Class 221 Super Voyagers and even a new Class 805 unit made using ready-to-run Bachmann and Hornby products as their basis respectively.

GRAND CHALLENGE

While all this was going on we hatched another plan. An innocent comment at the 2022 Great Electric Train Show and the question of how big could we make Making Tracks at the show lead to an answer we had never planned for – 152ft. Could we do it? We'd never designed the Making Tracks layout with a view to joining them together – in fact, we'd only started with a plan to do this once in 2021. But we saw the potential and loved the challenge. We were on – Making Tracks was going big for the 2023 Great Electric Train Show with a target of 152ft x 14ft titled The Grand Challenge.

Now the problems start. A 64ft self-contained layout is one thing, but how do you near triple the size and what problems will you encounter? For starters we had different electrical systems on each of the layouts which had to be resolved and secondly, we had to think about power. One booster running a circuit over 300ft long was never going to work.

What we hadn't bargained for were the actual challenges in being at one of the busiest model railway shows I've ever seen in the modern day – WIFI networks. There were so many networks in the show hall with stall holders, phone signals and the venue systems all fighting for space that it brought us to a stop on the Saturday morning. We worked through the problems, got everything up and running again and put on a brilliant show at an event we'll never forget.

The public were fascinated by Making Tracks, and it was incredible to see the 152ft layout unfold from the five Luton bodied vans and then somehow fit back in them all for the journey back to the workshop.

Through all of this I had been working with a TV production company in Manchester on a series for More Four on well-known people and model railways – *Little Trains and Big Names with Pete Waterman*. It was to be in four parts and for one reason or another took longer than expected to make but it was very successful and had some very funny moments.

In a conversation back in the workshop Mike told us they wanted to do a new type of show at the National Exhibition Centre for all modellers bringing together model railways, scale modelling, radio control and other genres. I had been pushing for this for a long time; I thought it would open lots of skills that we didn't use as the diorama models blow me away all be it less than a foot square and in our way was what we were trying to achieve. Then I made the mistake of saying something without engaging my brain… ■

That moment, you can see what it means from Pete's face as Pravin Patel hands over the official Guinness World Records certificate at Model World LIVE 2024. The Railnuts had done it – they had the World's Largest Portable Model Railway in history. *Jonathan Newton.*

The Final Frontier

PETE WATERMAN reflects on how a record-breaking layout helped steady the course of the UK model railway scene - reassuring manufacturers, inspiring modellers, and proving that teamwork, ambition and scenic detail still matter more than ever.

I had long been interested in the way the US modellers did shows where they meet and put their layouts together to make one massive railway for a weekend. What if we put all ours together?

Sometimes things happen that you don't give a thought to or even care about, and an odd conversation with More4 TV trying to explain how big it was led to a throwaway statement by me: "It's probably the biggest portable layout built at one time in the world." That started a few saying, "Can't be - there must be bigger in the States." I was sure of my facts, as I guessed no one else was as daft as us. A couple of the TV guys decided to look into it, and I thought no more about it. The next thing I knew, More4 thought it would be a great idea to go for the Guinness World Record.

We worked out that the new Model World LIVE event by Key Publishing at the National Exhibition Centre (NEC) would be the place, and Mike and his team launching the new

Gaining the world record called for engineering expertise. Tom and Daniel Rotherham were on hand to help design, build and prove their measuring device for the track length required for the world record. The process is explained to Guinness World Records' Pravin Patel at Model World LIVE 2024. *Jonathan Newton.*

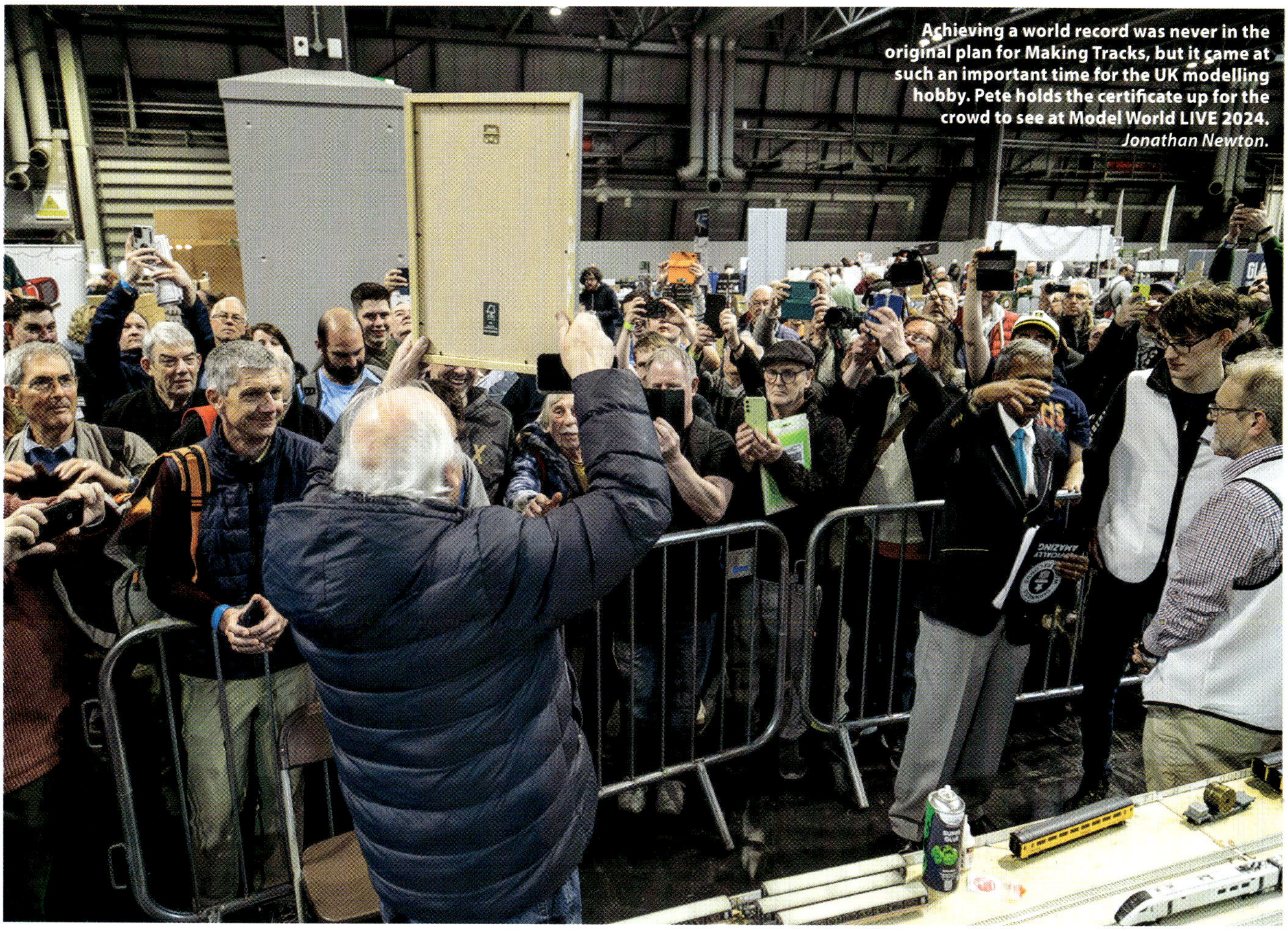

Achieving a world record was never in the original plan for Making Tracks, but it came at such an important time for the UK modelling hobby. Pete holds the certificate up for the crowd to see at Model World LIVE 2024. *Jonathan Newton.*

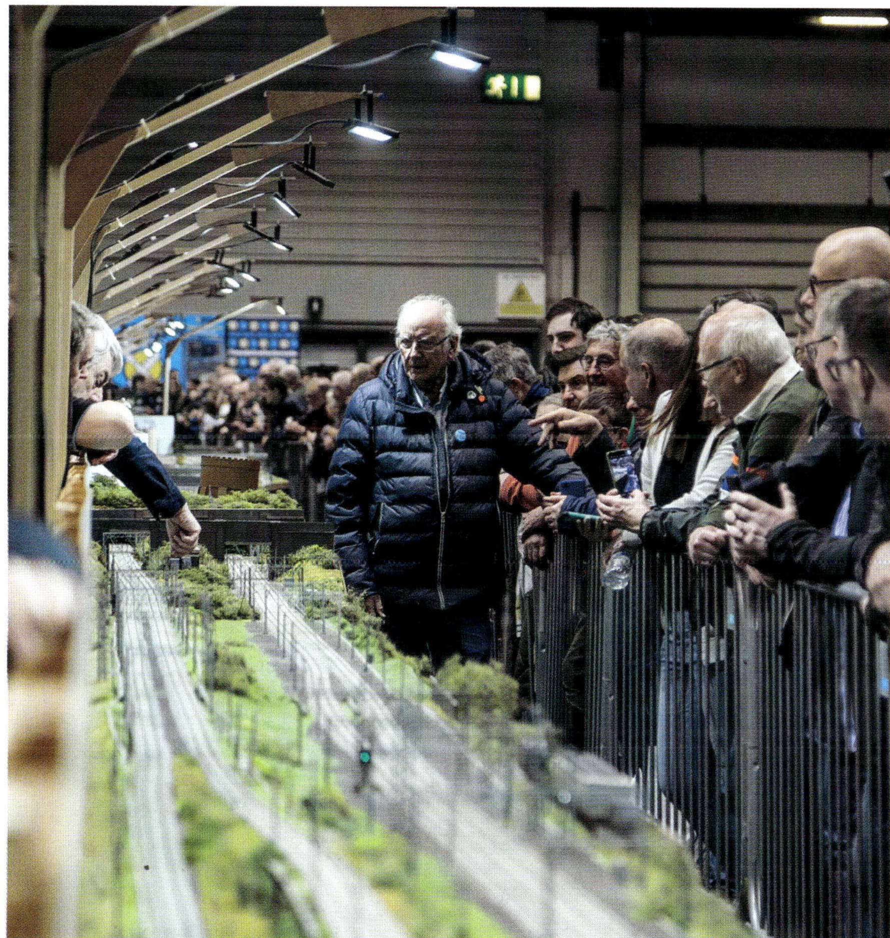

The expectant crowd looks on as Pete Waterman looks over Making Tracks the Final Frontier at Model World LIVE 2024. *Jonathan Newton.*

show were up for it - they could just fit in a 208ft long, 14ft wide layout. It was to be centre piece to this new show, but I hadn't appreciated how stressful it would be even getting it into the venue. I left the logistics and event planning with Mike.

At this point, I have to say it was Chris Clenton and More4 who should take all the credit. Yes, we had to build it, but I now know if they had told me how much work was involved, we would have stopped. But after the success of the Milton Keynes layout at the Great Electric Train Show, which was 152ft, I think we thought we could do anything.

We had part of Making Tracks 1, all of 2 and 3 - so that was 152ft of scenic boards and the same length of storage yard from the 2023 Great Electric Train Show layout. So, we had to build 56ft more of scenic boards and 56ft of storage yard in a limited timeframe.

We looked at what we could model to get to 208ft - start at Hillmorton Junction on Making Tracks 2, Rugby, and end in Kilsby Tunnel. First problem - on this 64ft layout from 2022, once in the tunnel, the track then goes round to the left into the storage yard, so this had to be remade to go straight on. We looked at putting Roade Cutting in here but couldn't make it work. I had worked out that the next big part would be Milton Keynes, so it was a case of how to get there.

After Kilsby Tunnel, the next tunnel is Stow, and this is before the Northampton line rejoins. After that you get Blisworth, so 16ft of that, then into Milton Keynes. We missed out Wolverton as it's on a curve. We had already decided the last station would be Watford, as that would be our Milton Keynes station equivalent at the end of the 208ft long scenic section. We would use parts of Making Tracks 1 for the rest including Tring Cutting and Northchurch Tunnel.

This was a full-on project, but Phil and I thought the storage yard was far too long – 208ft of plain line with nothing on it didn't feel right. "Let's go round the corner with Bushey Viaduct" I said. As we had not, to date, gone round a corner, we added Bushey Station and the Overground tracks, which we felt would be more interesting but boy what a challenge it would be, especially with six months to build now two stations – remember it was only 18 months before we didn't have any stations on a Making Tracks layout!

Dave locked himself away building baseboards and tables. At the same time, we were getting ready for our first annual Christmas show at Blakemere Village. So, as you can see, I was not focused on world records - I really wasn't. It was only a chance remark that Chris made that sort of made me aware they were working behind the scenes with More4.

The modelling didn't stop after the world record. Watford Junction became Making Tracks 4 in its own right and over summer-autumn 2024 gained a series of stunning high-rise flats as well as the station car park beyond the platforms. *Mike Wild.*

Bushey Viaduct made its debut on the world record layout as a link between Watford Juncton on one side and Bushey on the other. A Colas Rail Class 56 leads a rake of TEA tankers across the bridge which is modelled exactly on the prototype. *Mike Wild.*

World record complete, Pete signs the official show guide for a young visitor to Model World LIVE 2024. This is what it is all about – encouraging a new generation of modellers. *Jonathan Newton.*

We were going to build 208ft whatever, we had decided that, and that was our focus, and that fully engaged all of us. Phil was doing all the drawings and cutting the buildings, the rest of us laying track, ballasting, and all the scenic work. To say it was tight is an understatement. I then became aware of some of the problems Chris was having. The rules to get the record were very strict, and the measurements very accurate. You had to show how you calibrated your measurements and had to have qualified engineers to do this. Lucky for us, we had the twins – Tom and Daniel - both qualified aerospace technicians. They made a wagon that would measure every centimetre of track within a set tolerance.

TWO DAY BUILD

We had nowhere to put 208ft up before the NEC, and Mike had got us an extra day before the rest of the traders and layouts came in which gave us extra precious time without distractions to get the layout up. That first build day was essential – it was all about getting the layout into one piece, not about running trains – that would come on Friday, and it went well, until it didn't.

We'd loaded five vans with 54 8ft long baseboards, over 100 table legs and girders, all the buildings, equipment, scenic materials and then disaster! As we went to fit the last storage yard board, we realised we had packed the wrong one and there was no way of getting back to Warrington to change it. I would have to reconfigure this board. I needed track, but where from? There were no traders in the hall and who was closest? Mike jumped in and suggested Tony's Trains in Rugby. He phoned ahead to check Tony had what we needed, and I jumped in my car and went to Tony's Trains - and got a speeding ticket.

That didn't help the stress levels of what was already becoming a frantic day. It was 5.30pm when I got back, and it was 10pm on the Thursday before the track was finished and the layout was all together - and that was

The completed Watford Junction station makes a stunning addition to the layout. The team even added the Overground terminus platforms to the station on a new baseboard. *Mike Wild.*

"I was doing radio and television interviews like I had never done before, and I had to start again with BBC Breakfast at 6.30am."

PETE WATERMAN OBE

with help from some other layout owners who had come down early from Scotland to get set for the next day.

The stress had started. The next problem was the NEC switch the power off at midnight, I was unaware of this. I can only say while all this was going on I was doing radio and television interviews like I had never done before, and I had to start again with BBC Breakfast at 6.30am. The guys did a fantastic job getting something moving for the first part, but they were coming back to us live at 8.30am where the presenter was going to drive a train round the layout so the viewers could see just how big it really was. At the same time, the Guinness judge had started his scrutineering, and the public had entered at 9.30am with the boys frantically putting on a show, but the layout was still playing up.

What we had not figured was with Hattons Model Railways closing and the Warley National Model Railway Exhibition being cancelled in January was the impact that Making Tracks was about to have. We were here doing what we did at the NEC at Model World LIVE, a place which had become so familiar to us over the past 20 years as the Warley Show, but under a different name.

I didn't see what we were doing was having a major effect on the industry but by the time the show opened, I had been on *BBC Breakfast* – with two live broadcasts, I don't think I've ever seen that at a model railway show, *ITV News*, *Sky News*, and US networks. I had done over 60 radio interviews, and it was in most of the day's papers.

I could see that Phil was struggling with the electrics and Chris and the twins were having a torrid time with the man from Guinness. The place was packed, and everybody was wanting us to do it - as they say, the love in the room was fantastic.

We were due to make the announcement at 12:30, but due to some of the power problems, Chris and the team had not yet done all their measurements, so the announcement had to be put back. It had never dawned on me that we would not do it, but I could see the guys were starting to look worried. We were then asked to go into the office with the man from Guinness, who made a speech - which I did not quite take in - but I saw Mike and Chris's faces. He wanted it remeasured to see it again.

At that point, I'd had it - I had to go outside and sit on my own. I have never had to do this before. I just thought we could not let the hobby down - all the people who had turned up, all the media that were following us. What could I say? The boys had worked their socks

Bushey allowed main line trains to be seen out on the line, much like they had been on Making Tracks 1 and 2. Ultimately this scene will become part of Making Tracks 5. Here, an Accurascale Class 66 leads a rake of Revolution Trains HOA hoppers along the slow line. *Mike Wild.*

Expanding Making Tracks 4 into a layout of its own also meant building the distinctive station build at Watford Junction. This unique laser-cut kit was designed by Phil Moreton of PJM Models. *Mike Wild.*

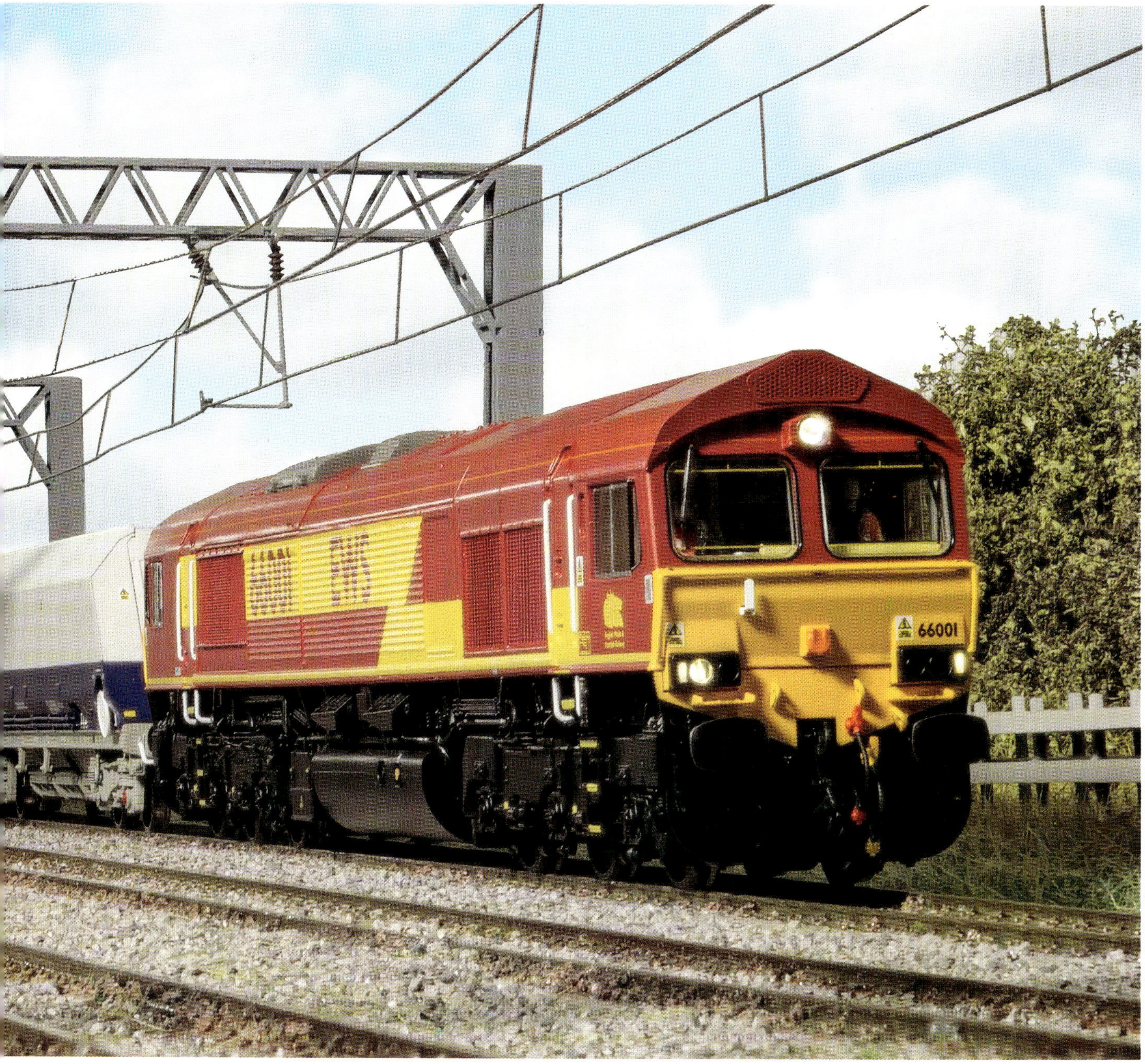

The first vision of the new flats in context with the station showed just how big they would be at Watford. ***Mike Wild.***

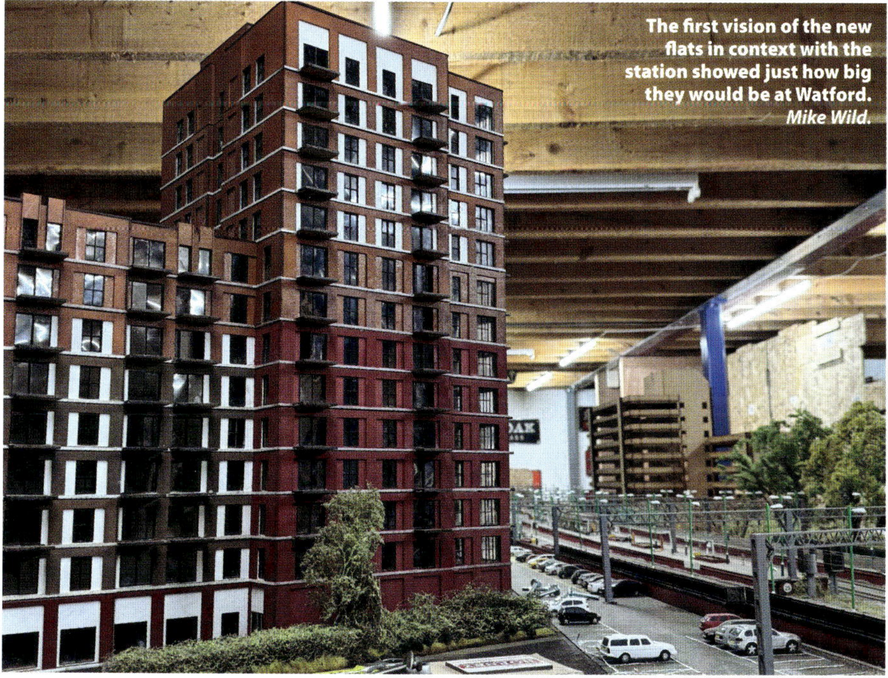

off. I felt very alone - it was as if I had the hobby on my back. Chris came and found me and said they were just finishing off.

As I walked back, I felt the tension. The TV guys asked me questions I couldn't answer. I can be honest and say I really did not know what was going on. It was as if everything was in slow motion. The next thing I was aware of - the crowd were going mad, and I was being handed the certificate. Simon from the TV crew asked me to say a few words - I just broke down. I couldn't speak; it had all been too much. People around me were holding me up and being so kind. How I stayed upright, I have no idea.

The rest of the Saturday was a blur. I did not hang around for all the photographs. I think I just walked around the exhibition looking at all the other things on show. Then the radio interviews started again. I've been in radio and television for over 40 years, so at last I was back in my comfort zone and could again take it all in and have a laugh at it all.

On the Sunday there were more radio interviews and at last it was fun. People

Few layouts can boast a housing estate, but 208ft long Making Tracks The Final Frontier had the space. Each was built from a PJM Models laser-cut kit based on structures seen on Tunnel Wood Road in Watford. *Mike Wild.*

were coming over to congratulate the gang, and the mood was fantastic. Everybody was so upbeat and enjoying themselves, the atmosphere was fantastic. And the effect of that World Record went beyond our shores – with such huge TV coverage it showed to the world just how big model railways were here in the UK.

I have to add here that I'm writing this article in the first person, but Making Tracks is not me, and Railnuts is not me. We are a group of people that work together. I may be the face and name you see, but it's the time and the volunteers that make this happen. A small group of us meet two days a week to build the layouts, and at shows we need lots of help. So this was their triumph, not mine - one man could not have done this, and more importantly, *should not have*. It's all about the team. They make the impossible possible.

REALISATION

The next day I was having a talk with one of the manufacturers, and he made a comment that brought home to me the scale of what the Railnuts had done in its Guinness World Record. What started out as an off-the-cuff statement had an industry effect that was amazing.

Although we live on a small island and can be quite insular, the hobby and its manufacturers are worldwide. Most of the

UK's rolling stock is made in China. The news that Hattons had closed and that Warley was cancelled had sent shockwaves around the world. All the broadsheets had carried the story plus Hornby's slowdown.

The factories in China expressed concern to UK companies about future production schedules, as recent news - including the closure of Hattons, the cancellation of Warley - had led to uncertainty about the stability of the UK model railway market.

I had offered to get the Warley show underwritten to take time to look at it, but there was not the will. And as much as I can see why, and did know the problems behind the show, Warley had become a flagship for our hobby - and one can argue that it was bigger than the Warley Model Railway Club. Indeed, was it fair that so much was put on so few? The loss of this event showed weakness in our hobby.

I pointed out how Railnuts is a team and how important it is to have a team. But you are not always going to agree on everything, and there will be personality clashes from time to time - but that's all part of life, not just model railways. You have to have succession, or it ends. We all get tired, and yes, we all get old. Yes, it's that word, old. We can't get up and down like we used to, we are a bit more crotchety, but we have to deal

with that, not anyone else.

WATFORD REMADE

With the World Record complete we returned to the workshop and planning for the summer 2024 Chester Cathedral layout. We only had three months to get the layout ready and what we came up with was that part of the record layout would be what we took for the summer.

Watford Junction was selected, but we soon realised it wasn't quite right. It looked like a country station where Watford is a busy city with huge tower blocks all around the station. We couldn't achieve those in three months, but what we did was to combine Bushey Viaduct, Watford Junction station and Watford Tunnel with a new scene modelling Roade Cutting to take the layout back to the storage yard at the back. For the first time Making Tracks had scenery around both ends which helped the fourth layout stand out.

Phil was keen to make Watford wider, like we had done for Milton Keynes, and I was keen to build the new flats that were being built to the east of the station as I had seen Rod Stewart's American 'HO' scale layout and loved the height that it modelled. "We could do something like that" I thought, as the Watford flats were up to 20 storeys tall and would make an amazing backdrop to the station.

It was decided that we would build the flats

Pete Waterman and Andy Goss build new floors for the flats at Chester Cathedral in summer 2024. *Phil Moreton.*

at the Cathedral to show how Phil's buildings worked and how easy they were to build. Andy Goss joined the team around that time and we spent our time building the flats and by the last week we had one 14 storey block ready to add – they were big projects!

I always thought that Milton Keynes was a one-off as far as we were concerned, but building the flats had really got us motivated. We saw this from the crowd reaction at the Great Electric Train Show in October 2024 as we showed Watford for the first time with two full sets of flats and, perhaps just as impressive, Watford Junction's station building office block. The response showed that we were on to something new.

The next outing was the Christmas event at Blakemere where we set up at the start of December, this was so we could work on the full layout as there's no space in the workshop for 64ft.

We had been working flat out since the Great Electric Train Show to get all three blocks of flats built and placed in their space at the back of Watford station. Phil really wanted to get the angle of the flats right, we got it, but didn't have exactly the right space and needed to rebuild the road bridge which passes across the north of the station.

Watford was looking the part, but also not quite. With Christmas over we were back in the

workshop to get the angle that Phil wanted as we had another 8ft which was going to be installed to make Watford 72ft long for its next outing at Model World LIVE 2025.

It's easy sometimes to say, 'just added an extra 8ft', but 8ft is only the length – we had a 5ft width to fill at the same time and when you realise, we can only get about 32ft up at a time in the workshop you start to see the challenges.

To build the new scene meant we could only have part of the station scene assembled with the next board after the 8ft – that's four 8ft long boards. We got all this assembled and then realised just how big of a challenge it was, as we had to remodel a 16ft x 3ft area behind the station scene as well as the new 8ft x 3ft section to extend Watford to 72ft.

I pass though Watford twice a week so know the place well. The task that faced me was how much scenic modelling had to be done. Phil had loved the big trees I had built for the front of the layout so I could do some big trees and a backdrop as we tried to model what in 8ft, after the new board, would have covered 64ft – a scale mile.

The new board had three blocks of flats, each one different to its neighbour and all very different to the new multi-storey towers we had built during 2024. Phil was very keen to do these, but they were a huge challenge at the design stage, never mind building them.

The new structures were smaller than the tallest structures, but so much more complex, and they all had to sit in an elevated position above the railway. It took three months just to design the most complex which has angled sides and I can assure you this 'small' 8ft extension was the straw that nearly broke the camel's back!

But it taught us all a lesson – if you want to get it right, it will take longer than you think.

It's fair to say this has changed our thinking. These three block are outstanding, I mean their detail is out of this world. But even though we had a whole day on the Thursday of Model World LIVE to ourselves we did not finish building structures until 8.30pm on the Friday night, just in time for the opening.

The feeling though when I walked in on Saturday morning and saw it as the public would I knew that Making Tracks would never be the same again - we had pushed the bar up to another level.

FOUR OR FIVE FOR '25

2025 would be our last year in the Cathedral and would have been Making Tracks 5's turn – our fifth layout! Phil and I were already on with it. Dave made all the boards so was well in front of us when I put the new board up for it and started on the scenery, but I could see that Phil was concerned.

> *"When Mike challenged us to build a station three years earlier, we had no idea how it would go."*

PETE WATERMAN OBE

We had long conversations about Wembley station which we could both see was a massive task - and that was only half of the job. At the other end was Bushey which needed two station buildings, a car dealership, an extension to the overground line and so much more scenery. With nine weeks to go it was too much work. I did lose sleep over it, but in the end, we decided we would do it right and if it took longer then so be it – that was the lesson we had learned.

The way we had built Watford over the shows showed us that if the railway runs and you add new features at each event, it's like you are taking a new layout out. The additions get noticed more and are a talking point, and I guess it serves two types of visitors: the ones that want to see trains running and those that want to see how it's done.

When Mike challenged us to build a station three years earlier, we had no idea how this would go. We have built not just one station, but four - and the whole area around them. Looking at it when we put it all together will have modelled from Rugby to Wembley that's 216ft x 14ft with 294ft of it fully scenic modelling - over nine scale miles of modelling. Just think how much ballasting that means!

LAST PROJECT

Making Tracks 5 will be our last major task in the Making Tracks story as we have run out of room to store any more, but it isn't the end for these layouts. Over the last five years we have been to 20 shows. I think we may be a bit tired, but the layout itself needs some updates.

One of the things has been the speed that we've had to build each part and how over these five years things have moved on. On the first layout we changed all the colour light signals by hand then Dave wired in a board he had made to make it automatic. He added it in front of the public and at times we did get some laughs when I came out from under the boards in a cloud of smoke with a soldering iron in my hand.

The first year I spent half my time putting the old ZIMO handsets back together which finally give up the ghost on the last day, it was the last train but then we were in a Cathedral. The wiring was always going to be a temporary thing as we never dreamed, we would be still doing this six years on. We now have to rewire all the layout as most of the problems we get are down to the wiring. This in itself is a massive undertaking with over 1200ft of cabling.

I've been modelling and playing trains for over 76 years as I come close to my 80th birthday I'm not planning to stop what has been a joy and sometimes a safe haven. See you at a show soon with Making Tracks. ■

Roade Cutting was a new addition to Making Tracks 4 to complete the circuit back to the rear storage yard. This complex brick lined cutting was modelled using bespoke laser-cut components created by PJM Models. *Mike Wild.*

NEW! PRE-ORDER NOW – COLAS RAIL 43277 AND 43257

Exclusive 'OO' gauge Hornby HST train pack featuring Colas Rail HST power cars

Key Publishing has commissioned Hornby to produce a brand-new limited edition for 'OO' gauge modelling Colas Rail operated Class 43 HST power cars 43277 *Safety Task Force* and 43257.

Highlights include:
- Unique livery artwork
- Limited to 400 units – 200 DCC ready, 200 DCC sound fitted
- 43277 *Safety Task Force* (powered) and 43257 (unpowered)
- Five-pole motor and twin flywheels
- 21-pin decoder socket in both power cars
- Digital sound option with Hornby TXS sound
- Independently powered roof fans

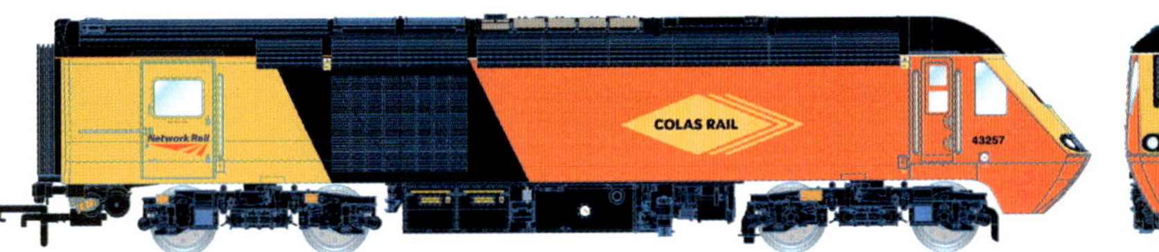

FULL PRICE: • **£394.99** DCC ready • **£449.99** DCC sound fitted
Order now to secure yours with a £30 non-refundable deposit

NEW! PRE-ORDER NOW – LMR 'WD' 600 *GORDON*

Clark Railworks Special Edition 'WD' 2-10-0 in 1960s condition

Clark Railworks is producing an exclusive Special Edition for Key Publishing modelling 'WD' 2-10-0 600 *Gordon* in its 1960s Longmoor Military Railway blue livery. The 'OO' gauge model is due to arrive in the fourth quarter of 2025.

Highlights include:
- Unique 1960s period livery artwork
- Special Edition of 250 units – 125 DCC ready, 125 DCC sound fitted
- Models 600 *Gordon* in 1960s LMR blue
- Coreless motor
- Die-cast, brass and plastic construction
- Digital sound option
- Firebox flicker

FULL PRICE: • **£295.00** DCC ready • **£425.00** DCC sound fitted
Order now to secure yours with a £30 non-refundable deposit

NEW! PRE-ORDER NOW – 56103 IN DCRAIL GREY

Exclusive Cavalex Models modern-era Class 56

New to the Key Publishing Exclusive limited edition collection is this Cavalex Models Class 56 modelling 56103 in DCRail grey with Devon Cornwall Railway roundels. Pre-order today to secure your model.

Highlights include:
- Unique livery artwork
- Limited to 300 units – 150 DCC ready, 150 DCC sound fitted
- Models 56103 in DCRail grey
- Five-pole motor and twin flywheels
- 21-pin decoder socket
- Digital sound option with ESU sound and speaker
- Independently powered roof fans

FULL PRICE: • **£189.95** DCC ready • **£289.95** DCC sound fitted
Order now to secure yours with a £30 non-refundable deposit

LAST FEW - IN STOCK NOW!
Exclusive Hornby CrossCountry HST Farewell pack

The remaining stock of our Hornby Class 43 HST pack featuring 43184 *Laira Diesel Depot* in retro InterCity Executive colours and 43366 *HST40* in CrossCountry livery is available now.

Highlights include:
- Unique livery artwork
- Limited to 350 units – 200 DCC ready, 150 DCC sound fitted
- Five-pole motor and twin flywheels in 43184
- Models of 43184 *Laira Diesel Depot* and 43366 *HST40*
- 21-pin decoder socket in both power cars
- Factory fitted 15mm x 11mm cube speakers
- Independently powered roof fans

FULL PRICE: • £359.99 DCC ready **• £399.99** DCC sound fitted

---

IN STOCK NOW! 47817 FOR 'OO'
Exclusive Heljan 'OO' gauge model of Porterbrook's Class 47

Our Heljan limited edition of Class 47 47817 in Porterbrook purple and white has arrived and features a bespoke purple and white box as well as an impressive specification.

Highlights include:
- Stunning Porterbrook purple and white livery
- Limited to 300 models
- Choice of DCC ready and DCC sound fitted models
- Powerful five-pole motor and twin flywheels
- Fully controllable lighting (on DCC)
- LokSound V5 21-pin decoder in DCC sound fitted models

FULL PRICE: • £199.95 DCC ready **• £299.95** DCC sound fitted

---

IN STOCK NOW! Bachmann Class 40 40145
Add a unique railtour locomotive to your fleet for 'OO' gauge

Our Bachmann limited edition of Class 40 40145 *East Lancashire Railway* in BR large logo blue is in stock and available now. This superbly presented model replicates the preserved 1Co-Co1 as it was between 2007 and 2010 on main line railtours.

Highlights include:
- Unique preservation era BR large logo blue livery
- Limited to 500 models
- Choice of DCC ready and DCC sound fitted models
- Powerful five-pole motor and twin flywheels
- Fully controllable lighting (on DCC)
- LokSound V5 Plux22 decoder in DCC sound fitted models

FULL PRICE: • £195.95 DCC ready **• £295.95** DCC sound fitted

---

CHECK OUT OUR FULL COLLECTION OF EXCLUSIVE MODELS HERE:
shop.keymodelworld.com

Modelling past, present and future

From gluing together kits in post-war Coventry to pioneering cutting-edge 'O' gauge models, **PETE WATERMAN** reflects on seven decades immersed in railway modelling. He shares how the hobby has evolved, what's been gained - and lost - along the way, and why Making Tracks marks both a proud milestone and a heartfelt connection to a lifelong passion.

I started modelling in earnest in 1955. In those days the choice was very limited, and it was very much a do-it-yourself hobby. You had to have a few different skills to be able to build models while the first Airfix kits had not long been on the market and glues were in their infancy.

A few of you will remember the horrible fish and bone glue in the electric pots we used in schools. We had woodwork, metalwork and art classes, Maths and Tech Drawing – what more could a modeller wish for?

Plastic was the new thing and, more importantly, there seemed to be a bit more money about, so you got a bit more pocket money. In Coventry there were a good six or seven model shops and, even if you had no money to buy what you wanted, you could press your nose up to the window and peer inside at what you could buy.

Of course, Christmas was the big thing, and you planned your big wishes round then, and maybe your birthday would bring you a wagon. The 1950s was about Hornby, Dinky and Tri-ang, Basset-Lowke and Trix. By the time I got the real bug of wanting to do more than send trains round and round, there were a couple of modelling magazines – the main one, and a must, was *Railway Modeller*. There was also a craft one by a company called MAP – small when compared with *Railway Modeller*, but it really was for the modeller, as it was part of what I would now call a do-it-yourself magazine.

Peco had a range of build-it-yourself wagons: Peco Wonderful Wagons. I have no idea how many of these I must have bought, but it was a way of helping finance my own layout, as I sold them on at the local model shop. The owner would give me the kits, I would build them, and I would get the kits that I needed for my layout in return for building them.

My bike did a lot of miles running around the model shops. There was always something that inspired you – be it in a magazine or in a shop. Buying a model in a box was out of the

Pete Waterman stands with his 'O' gauge model of Leamington Spa – his layout of a lifetime which recreates childhood spotting days in 7mm:1ft scale. *Mike Wild.*

question, so make it you had to. By the time I left school I had a lot of bits and pieces, but not a layout, as I still lived at home.

CHANGING WORLD

As I started working, I did have spare cash and the model world was changing. The first white metal kits were around, and the first model railway plastic kits started to pop up. Some were pretty basic but they were better than nothing. There was also a new magazine in the 1960s – *Model Railway Constructor* – this was along the lines of the *Railway Modeller*, and everything looked fantastic. Out on the big railway BR had its first electric blue electrics on the West Coast ushering in a new era of railway travel – the world looked great from my point of view as a new era started to bloom.

There was always someone in the model shops to give you advice, so they became the go-to place. There were local shows, but nothing on the scale we've come to know

today. But all this was about to change.

I hope you've picked up the frustration of modelling in the 1950s and 1960s – there was, and you could feel it, a lot of wanting to do more. Everything was just short of what you wanted when it came to quality. The wheelbase was a compromise, the track was too tight and overscale. Then came the revolution – Pendon, Roye England's inspired project to preserve the history of England in miniature.

Looking back from where we are now it's hard to say why this shocked modellers to the core. After all this time we now take scale models for granted, but back then this made us all rethink what we were doing. New technology has always pushed things forward, and etched brass was the new thing. A cottage industry grew up around it – small manufacturers making scale model kits that looked like the engines Guy Williams of Pendon was building.

Recreating the BR steam era, a pair of Just Like the Real Thing kit-built GWR 'Castle' 4-6-0s storm out of the tunnel onto Hatton Bank on Pete Waterman's 'O' gauge layout. *Mike Wild.*

This led to a different type of model railway show on a national level – a place you had to go to get your bits and see what was on offer and how others were making models and moving the hobby forward. At the same time the layouts at these shows changed – scale was now the thing. It had to look right and work like the real thing – realism was the key. People became evangelists of scale, but for most of us we ploughed the middle ground.

What had started off as shows to help raise money for a local club now changed to bigger clubs putting on big shows in big venues like York, Bristol and Central Hall London. At the same time we saw the birth of scale shows – these were very small – but that's the Pendon effect, and I can still see that effect today – yes, today!

BOOM TIME

Was the hobby booming and did it have anywhere to go? Well, I don't think anyone would have seen what was about to happen.

At the time, Tri-ang had bought Hornby and rebranded it. The kit manufacturers were K's, Wills and Ratio. Peco had the magazine to read and its track system. But, as always, things are never what you see on the surface.

From my viewpoint, it looked great – by the 1970s we had our own kits at Models and Leisure, which we could not make enough of. OPC books were driving interest – everybody seemed to have the volumes of GWR engines. What was there not to like? The *Railway*

Modeller's strapline was For The Average Modeller! Who wanted to be the average anything? I, along with a lot, had lost sight of what the hobby was.

We soon got brought down to earth when two new manufacturers from China announced they were entering the UK market – Airfix and Mainline – and when we saw their product: wow. It was nothing short of sensational. Now what we were offering as a kit was available to every modeller in a box ready-to-run and at a good price, and boy,

did they sell. The shops could not get enough stock. So now we had three ready-to-run lines and the two new companies raised the bar significantly. It was the 1980s now and many of us still saw the rebranded Hornby as carrying the legacy of Tri-ang, both in style and perception while the new order brought in new ways of making models and from a different source too.

The hobby had never had it so good - great ready-to-run and great kits. What more could we wish for? Then two more names came into

Pete Waterman and Dave Douglas install points on Making Tracks 3. *Mike Wild.*

"The hobby had never had it so good - great ready-to-run and great kits. What more could we wish for?"

PETE WATERMAN

the market: Lima and Rivarossi. Wow. From the outside it looked fantastic, but the shops saw it from another angle, how much money could they have tied up in stock? Yes, there had been a rush back to the hobby with the new GWR locomotives, but now the rush was over, and the new announcements of new models were coming thick and fast.

It was the mid-1980s now and at the Toy Fair in January the two new companies showed their new models. On closer inspection I spotted they were kits built up and being advertised as pre-production models. The shops quickly realised that the products on display were early prototypes, and ultimately, those particular models didn't reach production.

In all the years I've been modelling, I've seen it all. We now have more manufacturers than ever before in the ready-to-run market for 'OO' gauge, with quality we haven't had and, at one time, could not have imagined. We see the stores entering the range game – we know also how that ends up. I've also seen what too much new stock means to the marketplace.

FINAL PROJECT

When we started Making Tracks back in 2020, we had been building Leamington in 'O' gauge for 20 years. I had had to go into manufacturing with Just Like the Real Thing

In the early days of Leamington Spa Pete aligns the curves on the Great Western lines on the approach to the station. *Pete Waterman Collection.*

Pete Waterman stands with the Just Like the Real Thing team in 2004. *Pete Waterman Collection.*

The Making Tracks team make progress on Hillmorton Junction for Making Tracks 2 in January 2022. *Richard Watson.*

The continual improvement of ready-to-run models has brought levels of detail that would have been unthinkable 70 years ago. An Accurascale Class 92 poses with a rake of Revolution Trains IPA car carriers in the developing Milton Keynes Central station in 2023. *Richard Watson.*

to get the models we needed for Leamington because they didn't exist. We knew it was a niche market, and we would not get reach, but we did think we could provide a good product at a fair price. It was a revolution for the 'O' gauge market. Some people embraced it, others didn't as we brought 3D printing, laser-cut wood and plastic, white metal parts and resin and plastic together.

Our stand stood out at the 'O' gauge shows and soon the word was that the future is 'O' gauge and ready-to-run. I remember only too well a Sunday morning at the workshop arguing with a couple of the guys that they would rue the day.

As we at Making Tracks start on what will have to be our last project – our age has a lot to do with it, but also we're out of space in the workshop – I find myself wanting to get back to my first love, 'O' gauge. There is still a fair bit to do – and yes, it really needs playing with too. What's the point in putting in all that effort if you don't run and enjoy it? It gives me the chance to run trains I remember from my youth and enjoy the company of like-minded people and friends. We're not competitive in any shape or form – we all do our best at what we choose. We're not judgmental – there's no "I wouldn't have done it like that", but a "Have you tried this?" or "Have you seen this?" Age brings with it knowledge – not all of it good, but it can get you thinking.

If we take laser-cut wood kits – they are fantastic and cheap, but they're not all great, and as always, you get what you pay for. Just because you bought a bad one, that doesn't mean they're all like that. If you get a good one – tell people about it. And if it's not – keep quiet.

There has been one company that's been the rock of British modelling, and that's Peco – and their role cannot be stated enough. I hate to think what the hobby would be like without them. They're still a family-run business yet its range of track products are the bedrock of model railways across the globe. That's an incredible achievement.

One of the biggest things that has changed everything is superglue. But like everything in life – they're not all the same, and in general, there's not a one-fits-all. Superglues are worth finding out about – they are far more interesting than you would think. I have soldered all my life – as a telephone engineer I had to. All my first kits had to be soldered, so from the start I understood flux, temperature and solder content. Well, it's the same with superglues – different types for different jobs.

BUSHEY TO WEMBLEY

Bushey to Wembley will be the last of the Making Tracks layouts, and we want this to be

Peco has had a lasting effect on the model railway hobby with its track system being used across the globe. Pete Waterman and the Making Tracks team lays Peco code 75 flexible track through Milton Keynes Central station in January 2023. *Mike Wild.*

Changes in the hobby have brought about new levels of detail in laser-cutting and 3D printing. Both technologies are enhancing the potential of the hobby. *Mike Wild.*

Pete Waterman works on one of the many bespoke 3D printed signals for Making Tracks 3. Another example of just how far the hobby has come and how working with a team makes the impossible possible. *Jonathan Newton.*

very special. Just the buildings alone on this section will be different – as we build our first hotel! When we take out this layout, there will be more buildings than railway! The workshop looks like the set from *Raiders of the Lost Ark* – there are that many packing boxes.

So here we are – over 70 years of modelling and doing without even thinking about it what started it all off for us: doing our own version of Pendon. Not 1930s Vale of the White Horse, but 2025 West Coast. But more than that – building what people know and love and taking it out for others to enjoy. For Pendon, it was a time gone by – for us it's the Here and Now.

Making Tracks is about entertaining and having fun and engagement and there's nothing better than seeing the smile on peoples faces as we hand them the controls to drive a train around one of the Making Tracks layouts. It's pure joy and has been a driving factor in making these layouts as popular as they are by making them accessible and offering everyone and anyone the chance to drive a model train. It's addictive you know!

This hobby should be for everyone to enjoy, and should give enjoyment – and I hope everyone can be good at something, if you let them. I have learnt one great lesson in life – never say never. We can do what we think we can't if we're part of a team.

Through this publication I have used I in lots of places because I'm writing it, but none of this would have happened without the fantastic people who help to make the dreams become reality. My skill, if indeed I have one, is putting teams of people together to achieve the impossible - yes the impossible: tell me I can't do it and I will show you how I can with a team of dedicated people. With that you can do anything.

My thanks to all those people that have made my life a dream. You all know who you are.

Happy modelling. ◼

BOOK NOW & SAVE!

THE
.GREAT ELECTRIC.
TRAIN SHOW

OCTOBER 11/12 2025

AT: ARENA MK, MILTON KEYNES
MK1 1ST

Join us for a spectacular weekend of railway modelling including Pete Waterman's 64ft long Making Tracks layout modelling the four-track West Coast Main Line in 'OO' gauge in the present day under the wires!

EVENT HIGHLIGHTS

THE BEST LAYOUTS – Inspire your own modelling with some of the best model railways featured in Hornby Magazine including the outstanding Grantham the Streamliner Years in 'OO', Folly Lane in 'OO' (HM202), Mothecombe in 'OO' and more across 'N', 'OO' and 'O' gauges.

QUALITY TRADE STANDS – Pick up the latest releases, specialist accessories, unique 3D printed products and more from our extensive range of trade stands including manufacturers and retailers.

BOOK NOW AND SAVE TODAY!
ADVANCE TICKETS ON SALE NOW

Buy your tickets before the show to get the best prices AND early access from 9.30am each day. On the day ticket prices £22 adults, £11 children (free entry for children on Sunday*).

✓ 30+ layouts
✓ 40+ traders
✓ Demonstrations
✓ Refreshments
✓ FREE shuttle bus from Milton Keynes Central station

OPEN:
Saturday: 10am-5pm
Sunday: 10am-4pm
Advance ticket holders get early entry from 9.30am

THE
.GREAT ELECTRIC.
TRAIN SHOW
Sponsored by:
accurascale
EllisClark TRAINS
DCC TRAIN AUTOMATION
DCCconcepts
thinking outside the square
WEST HILL WAGON WORKS

For full event details and advance tickets visit:
keymodelworld.com/greatelectrictrainshow

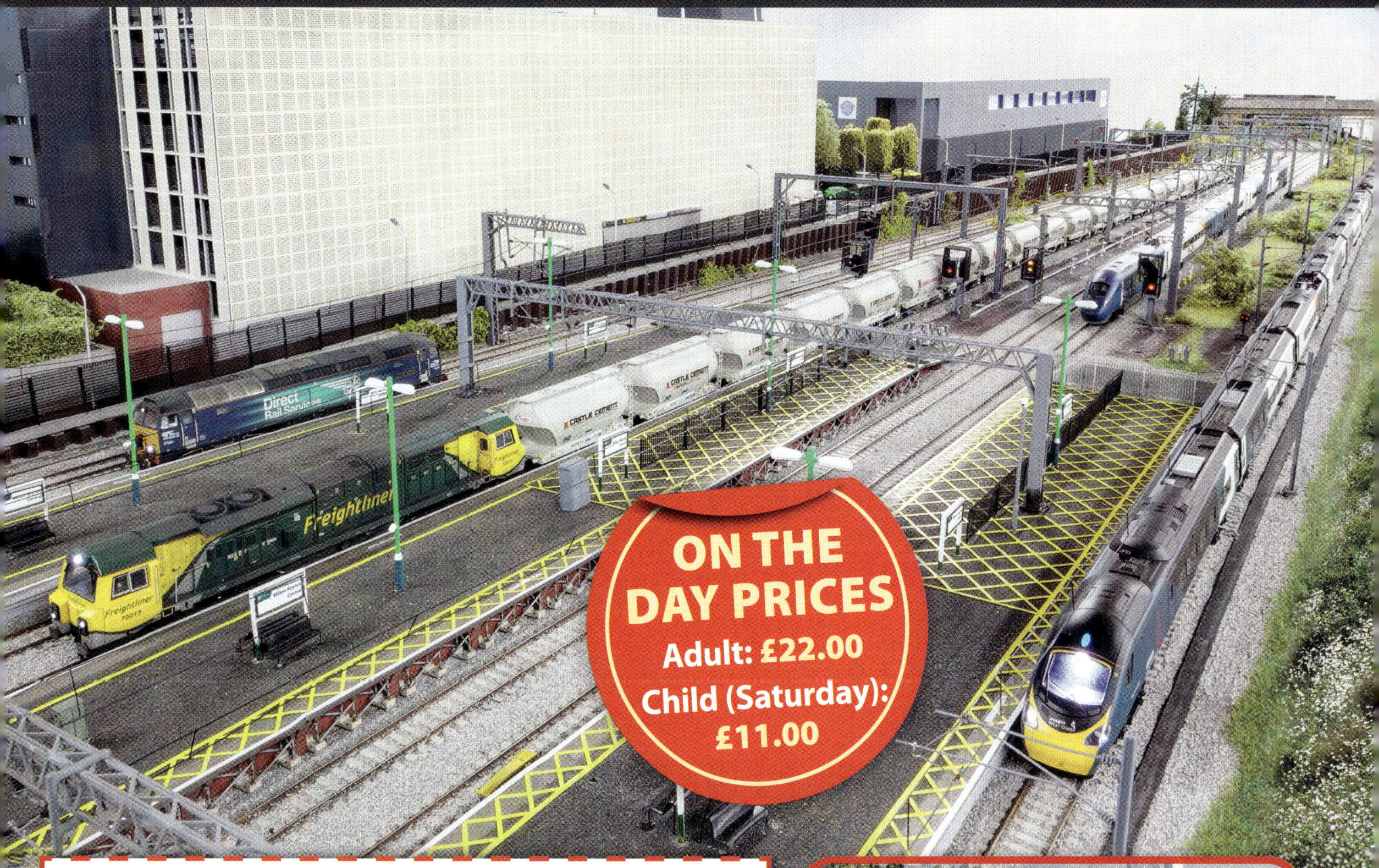

ON THE DAY PRICES
Adult: £22.00
Child (Saturday): £11.00

BUY ADVANCE TICKETS & SAVE!

Advance VIP ticket £55*

SATURDAY

- Advance adult subscriber £15.00
- Advance standard adult £17.00
- Advance child £9.00

SUNDAY**

- Advance adult subscriber £15.00
- Advance standard adult £17.00

*VIP Ticket includes a standard show admission ticket for both days, early entry, £25 of Key Publishing magazines and a sheet of discount vouchers to use at the show.

**Children 16 and under go FREE on Sunday, but must be accompanied by a paying adult. Maximum of two free children with each paying adult.

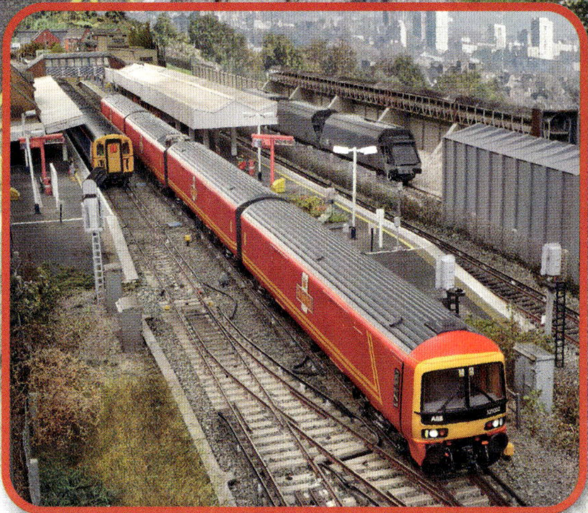

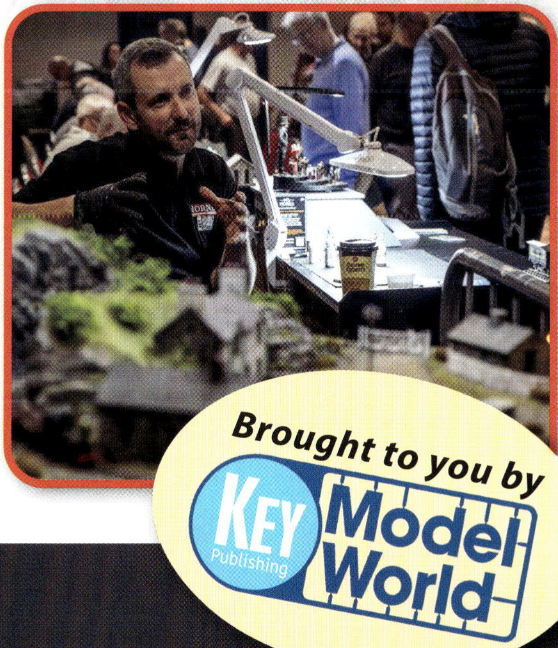

Brought to you by KEY Publishing Model World

Call 01780 480404

to book your advance tickets now and save!

713/25

THE DESTINATION FOR
RAIL MODELLING ENTHUSIASTS

Visit us today and discover all our latest releases

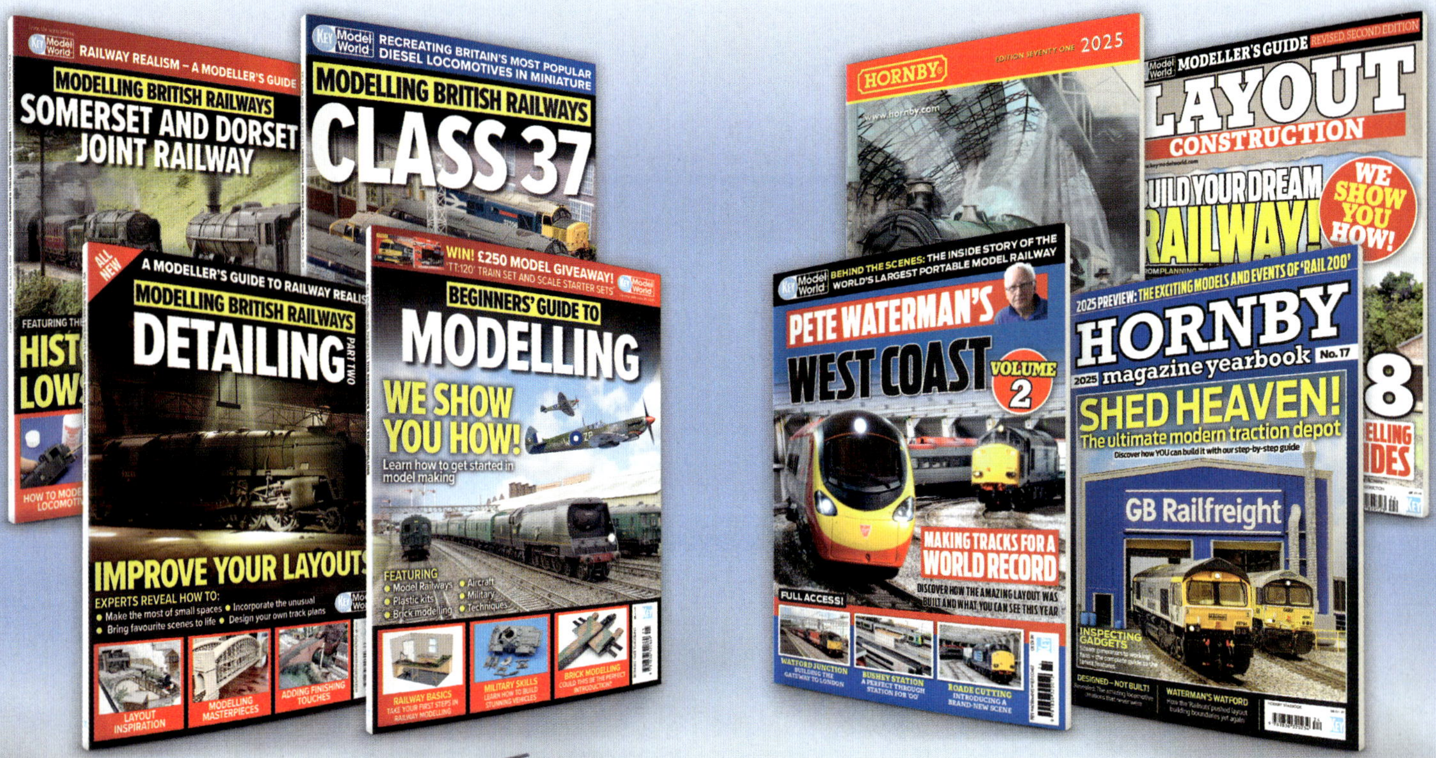

Order from our online shop today...
shop.keymodelworld.com/specials
Call +44 (0)1780 480404 *(Monday to Friday 9am - 5.30pm GMT)*
Free 2nd class P&P on BFPO orders. Overseas charges apply.

714/2

A TRADITIONAL SET - REIMAGINED

Relive those wonderful halcyon and imaginative days of the 1960s with this '00' gauge Tri-ang Railways Remembered Train Set. Consisting of a Class 3F 'Jinty' No. 47606 locomotive in a BR Black livery, two LMS Crimson passenger coaches, 1st radius starter oval, power clip and uncoupling ramp.

With a limited run of just 1000 sets, do not miss your chance to enjoy this little bit of nostalgia once again.

R1287M Tri-ang Railways Remembered: R2X Analogue Train Set

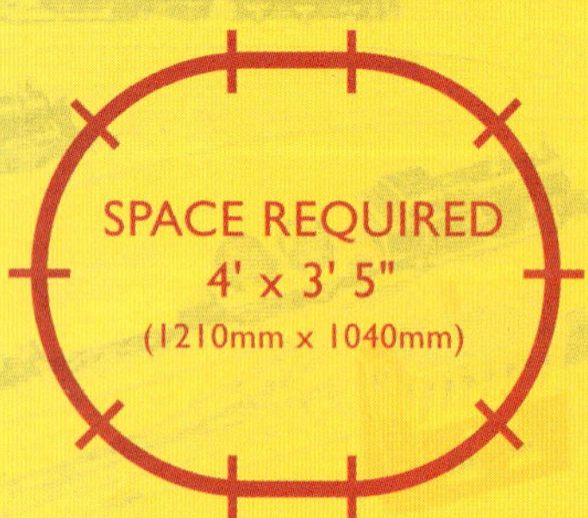

For more information please visit your local Hornby stockist or go to **hornby.com**

 Hornby Model Railways
 hornby
 officialhornby
 officialhornby
 hornbymodelrailways